Community First
Economics

By Jon Kiper

Copyright © 2025 by Jon Kiper. All rights reserved.

ISBN: 979-8-9878421-2-6

Softcover

Version 2.0

CommunityFirstEconomics.com

Published by Jay Bee Eye LLC

Cover Photo by Emily Butzer

Cover Design by Charles Lockwood

Thank you to Charles, Oscar, Stella, Emily, Dad,
and everyone else who helped with this book.

This book is dedicated to my son Ollie
and to all the children of the class of 2034.

Table of Contents

Introduction: Democracy is a Conversation
Chapter 1: The Big Kahuna
Chapter 2: What is Community First Economics?
Chapter 3: The Disappearing Middle Class
Chapter 4: The Housing Crisis & The Path Home
Chapter 5: The Property Tax & A Fair Funding System
Chapter 6: The Myth of the Self-Made Millionaire & The Rise of the Corporation
Chapter 7: The Price of Democracy
Chapter 8: Education as the Engine & Child Well-Being as Economic Policy
Chapter 9: How Health Care Became a Corporate System and How We Take It Back
Chapter 10: A New Social Contract: From GDP to Gross National Happiness
The End: Closing Jonny Boston's
General Further Exploration

Introduction

Democracy is a conversation. As a restaurant owner, I have had the privilege of having thousands of conversations over the last ten years. I have had long talks with customers from many political backgrounds, sometimes arguing over the bar late into the night.

What has surprised me is how often everything comes down to the same handful of issues. It does not matter whether the person is a Democrat, a Republican, or an Independent. When we talk about life, the same problems keep coming up: housing, childcare, healthcare, schools, aging, and basic community stability.

This book is a living document. I plan to update and expand it as we learn new information and gain new insight.

In the following pages, I have done my best to diagnose the big issues in our state while also offering some tangible solutions. Many ideas in this book have a long history and people in other times and places have used different names for some of the ideas I've proposed. I am not claiming to invent all of these ideas. What I am doing is translating hundreds of hours of discussions into a simple framework that people would understand. Now, we can finally see we're all talking about the same future. A future worth fighting for.

Chapter 1: The Big Kahuna

For ten years, I ran a restaurant in Newmarket, New Hampshire, called Jonny Boston's International. The name of the restaurant came from the years I spent living in Australia. When I got 'Down undah' after graduating from high school, I would tell people I was from "North of Boston…" "Oh so you're from Boston?" They'd say. "No." I'd say. "I'm from New Hampshire, it's North of Boston…" "Oh so you're from Boston then?"

Australians love nicknames, so I quickly became Jonny Boston. Later, when I spent a winter in Mexico, my roommate Jose´ would call me (after a little too much tequila), "Jonny Boston International! Jonny Boston Inter-Nation-Alllll!" Each syllable heavily exaggerated like a Mexican football commentator yelling GOAL!

So, in 2014, when I decided to open a restaurant serving international street food I thought it would be fun to reprise the role of Jonny Boston.

My restaurant was small, just 20 seats. At most, I had 6 employees, many of them high school kids, who only worked a few hours a week. It was from this humble position that I came to understand how the economy works on the most basic level.

One lesson I learned was the interconnectedness of the downtown businesses. If the hairdresser across the street was having a slow week, she wouldn't be in for margaritas after she closed. If the tattoo shop down the road was busy, the boss would order lunch for everyone. When the engineering firm down the road got sold, everyone got laid off, and we sold three fewer burritos every day.

The most important lesson though, came from one of our regulars, we called him, The Big Kahuna.

He wanted a burger that wasn't on the menu: a cheeseburger topped with pulled pork, barbecue sauce, a fried egg, cheddar cheese, and Sriracha. "I don't care what it costs," he said. It was so good, I put it on the menu and named it The Big Kahuna.

For most of the year, he'd come in maybe once a month. But in November, he started showing up several times a week. A few days before Christmas, I finally asked him why.

"I work at Best Buy," he explained. "Most of the year they only give me twenty hours a week." "That's odd." I said, "It's so they don't have to give me benefits. But around the holidays they give me more hours. When I get more hours, I can come here more."

Then he looked at me and said the line I've never forgotten: "If they *paid me more, I'd eat here more.*"

That was it. So simple. Just the truth. When working people have money, they spend it where they live; at my restaurant, the local café, the barber shop, the music venue. That daily spending is what keeps a town's heart beating. The Big Kahuna wasn't describing a radical idea. He was pointing out how a community's economy is supposed to work; a simple, powerful cycle that's been broken.

The Big Kahuna wasn't just talking about buying a burger. He was talking about belonging. About the simple human connection of being a regular somewhere, of being known, of supporting a local business and sharing a meal with neighbors. His ability to pursue that small, essential piece of the good life was dictated by the profit margin of a distant corporation.

For more than forty years our state and our country have operated under Ronald Reagan's promise that if we cut taxes for the wealthy and the corporations they own, the benefits would "trickle down" to everyone. Trickle-down economics has been the defining economic paradigm of my life.

But look at the results.

My dad supported our family of six on one engineer's salary in the 1990s. Today, in the same state, two incomes often aren't enough. He wasn't an outlier: in 1971, 61% of Americans lived in middle-class households, many supported by a single income. By 2021, that share had fallen to just 50%. I've been searching for an affordable home for my own family for nearly nine years.

Every year, I watch younger customers, friends, and even fellow small business owners get priced out, sometimes leaving New Hampshire altogether. Our property taxes keep climbing, funding our schools based on a town's wealth, not a child's future. Today, the poorest 20% of New Hampshire households pay about 8.9% of their income in taxes, while the richest 1% pay about 2.8%. We're working harder than ever but falling behind.

The old political fight, left versus right, big government versus small government, offers no new path forward. Trickle-down economics doesn't help the single mom working two jobs just to keep a roof over her family's head. It doesn't help the retiree who is being pushed out of the mobile home park because of property tax increases. It doesn't help the young person stuck in their parents' basement, wondering if they'll ever have a chance for a home of their own.

This book is built on a different idea, one I learned from my grill, my customers, and my own struggle to build a life here. It starts by reclaiming a phrase we've all heard but rarely stop to truly consider: the pursuit of happiness.

When Thomas Jefferson placed "the pursuit of Happiness" alongside Life and Liberty in the Declaration of Independence, he wasn't being poetic. He was being intentional. He was drawing on an Enlightenment idea, articulated by thinkers like John Locke, that the ultimate purpose of government is to create the conditions for human prosperity, what the Greeks called eudaimonia. This isn't fleeting pleasure or casual contentment. It's the deep, enduring satisfaction that comes from a life of meaning, connection, and dignity. It's the ability to raise a family in security, to contribute to your community, to have a stake in the future, and to know your children will have the same chance you did.

Jefferson and the founders understood that you cannot pursue happiness if you are exhausted, isolated, or one crisis away from homelessness. You pursue it on a foundation. That foundation is built of stable homes, great schools, reliable healthcare, trusted neighbors, and a shared stake in the future. It is built in **community**.

When that foundation crumbles, the pursuit of happiness becomes a luxury for the lucky few. For everyone else, it's just a meaningless quote on an old piece of paper.

Community First Economics is the practical philosophy of rebuilding that foundation: it recognizes that our fates are linked. My child's good school makes your town safer. Your secure retirement stabilizes our local economy. Our clean water ensures our collective health. Prosperity doesn't trickle down from the top. It is built from the middle out and the ground up, in strong communities.

This book isn't about left or right. It's about forward. It's a call to remember that the word "economy" comes from the Greek *oikonomia*: **"management of the household."** Our towns and state are our shared household. It's time we started managing it for the well-being, the happiness, of everyone who lives here.

The path forward demands that we put the needs of our towns ahead of corporate lobbyists and tired arguments about tradition. This is the only path that leads to a New Hampshire where people like The Big Kahuna, have the foundation to build a good life, raise a family, and pursue happiness with freedom and dignity.

That's the future worth fighting for. Let's get to work.

Chapter 2:
What is Community First Economics?

> "The greatness of a community is most accurately measured by the compassionate actions of its members."
> – Coretta Scott King

The story of The Big Kahuna points to a simple truth we've lost: an economy is healthy when money circulates. Money is like blood, and it needs to move around in a healthy body. But what is the goal?

For decades, our economic policy has been designed to make that money pool at the top, not flow. They called it "trickle-down," and we've been waiting for the drip ever since. Between 1979 and 2021, productivity in the U.S. grew by 65%, while hourly pay for typical workers grew by only 17%. The money didn't trickle down, it got vacuumed upward.

Community First Economics starts from a different, foundational principle: **the purpose of an economy is to enable the pursuit of happiness.**

That phrase from our Declaration of Independence is the operating instruction for a free society. It names the ultimate goal of these United

States. And you cannot pursue happiness if you're drowning in rent, terrified by medical bills, or working three jobs just to keep the lights on. **In New Hampshire today, 51% of renters are "cost-burdened," meaning they spend more than 30% of their income on housing.** You cannot pursue happiness in a community stripped of its main street businesses, its shared spaces, or its sense of common future.

When I first moved to Newmarket in 2010, I was paying $595 to live in a one-bedroom apartment. I split that with my girlfriend. Later we moved into a house with roommates and a yard, but never paid more than $600 for rent. When my son was born, we lived in a two-bedroom apartment (before we bought the building the restaurant is in) that cost $950. That was 2015. Today that same apartment is $2200. Young people are routinely paying double or triple what I was paying just 10 years ago.

The Failed Promise of Trickle-Down

Trickle-down economics, the governing economic philosophy of the last forty years, has a simple premise. The theory goes that if we cut taxes for the wealthy and for corporations, reduce regulations, and let capital move freely, the rich will use that extra money to invest, innovate, and create jobs. The benefits of their enriched activity will then, like water dripping through cracks, eventually "trickle down" to workers in the form of higher wages and to everyone in the form of a booming economy.

But the story was a fairy tale. The reality has been a major transfer of wealth from the middle-class to the rich. Since the major trickle-down tax cuts began:

•The wages for the top 1% have skyrocketed 171.7% since 1979 while bottom 90% wages have seen just 32.9% growth.

•The share of national income going to the top 1% has risen to over 20%.

•CEO pay has grown by 1,460% since 1978, while typical worker pay has grown just 18% (adjusted for inflation).

In a 2020 RAND Corporation study, researchers estimated that if incomes for the bottom ninety percent had grown at the pace of the overall economy since 1975, they would have earned about 2.5 trillion dollars more in 2018 alone. They would have earned about 47 trillion dollars more in total from 1975 to 2018. In plain terms, a huge share of economic growth that used to lift typical families has flowed upward for decades.

Why? Because the trickle-down theory was flawed. The wealthy didn't reinvest most of their windfalls in productive Main Street businesses or worker pay. They invested in financial assets, stock buybacks, mergers, and real estate, which further inflate the wealth of those who already own assets, driving inequality. In 2022 alone, S&P 500 companies spent over $922.7 billion on stock buybacks, money that could have raised every employee's salary by thousands of dollars.

We were sold a philosophy of growth, but what we got was a system of extraction. Community First Economics starts from the opposite, evidence-based principle: true prosperity doesn't trickle down, it is built from the ground up, in the financial strength and security of everyday people and the towns they call home.

Chapter 3:
The Disappearing Middle Class

"The anger in America comes from a simple truth: the middle class no longer believes that the system works for them. And too often, they're right." – Paul Krugman

The Erosion of the Stability

Growing up, my father worked as a nuclear engineer at the Seabrook power station. We lived in a modest house in a good school district. My mother stayed home with me and my three siblings. She was there when we left for school and when we got home. To make a little extra money, she'd babysit or sell crafts, but she didn't have a job until we were all in high school.

This wasn't unusual. Nearly all my friends lived in a similar household. One parent working, one parent at home. No one was rich, but no one was terrified, either. The math of life simply worked. There was a **foundation of stability** that allowed for the ordinary pursuits of happiness: family time, weekend projects, Little League games, saving for college, planning for retirement.

That world is gone. In the 1950s, 50% of households with children had a stay-at-home parent. By 2022, that number had fallen to 18%. For married couples, the sole breadwinner model dropped from 49% to 23%. For my generation, and for the one after, that basic stability has vanished. The middle class is the social bedrock that made 20th-century America a place of unprecedented prosperity, and it is disappearing. And its disappearance isn't an accident. It's the direct result of an economy we designed to extract value for capital first, and to nurture the foundations for human potential last.

When the Math Stopped Adding Up

For decades, the American promise was straightforward: work hard, play by the rules, and you'll earn a stable life. You could support a family, own a home, and give your kids a shot at something better on a single income. In New Hampshire, that meant a teacher, a mill worker, or a shopkeeper could be the bedrock of a community. Their labor provided more than just goods and services, but the very stability **upon which community life was built.**

Today, that bedrock is crumbling. Wages for most people have flatlined, while the cost of everything that defines a middle-class life has exploded.

Let's break down the new, impossible math:

Housing: In many New Hampshire towns, home prices have doubled or tripled in twenty years. Wages haven't come close. The median sales price of a home in New Hampshire rose from $127,500 in 1998 to $514,000 in 2024, which is about a **303% increase**. Median household income in the state grew by only 23% in the same period. The average rent now consumes a crippling share of a family's income, turning shelter from a source of security into a source of chronic anxiety.

Healthcare: Premiums and deductibles rise every year, turning medical care into a source of debt. In 2000, the average annual premium for employer-sponsored family health coverage was $6,438. By 2023, it was $23,968, a 272% increase, while inflation rose only 78%.

Childcare: For many families, the cost of full-time childcare is a second mortgage, if they can find a spot at all. In New Hampshire, the average annual cost of infant care is over $17,250, more than in-state tuition at UNH. This is a tax on parenthood.

Education: Once the ticket to the middle class, a college degree now comes with a debt sentence that pushes the dreams of homeownership, family, and career exploration out by a decade or more. The average student loan debt for New Hampshire graduates is over $39,000, the highest in the nation.

The result of this is even households with two working parents are barely getting by. They earn more, but they own less, save less, and feel less secure than their one-income parents did. The goalposts of a stable life aren't just moving, they're being blown away, and with them goes the mental and emotional space required to pursue anything beyond mere survival.

The Two-Income Trap

"The irony is that families are actually making more money today than they did a generation ago. The problem is that so are their creditors. The entire gain—plus a lot more—has been swallowed up by the banks, the mortgage companies, and the credit card companies."- *The Two-Income Trap: Why Middle-Class Parents Are Going Broke*

This is the great, unspoken swindle of the modern economy. My parents' generation saw a second income as a path upward, extra money for vacations, savings, or a nicer car. For my generation, a second income is the price just to stay afloat.

This "two-income trap" isn't just a personal stressor. It's a community-wide drain on the capacity for happiness.

Vulnerability: A family needs two incomes to survive: lose one job, and the whole house of cards collapses. Today, 37% of Americans can't cover a **$400** emergency. There's no cushion, no stay-at-home parent who can temporarily enter the workforce to bridge the gap. This creates a constant, low-grade terror that poisons well-being.

Time Poverty: Parents have less time for their kids, for PTA meetings, for coaching Little League, or for checking in on an elderly neighbor. Married parents with children now spend an additional 11 more hours per week on paid work than they did in 1975, time directly stripped from home and community. We outsource childhood to expensive daycare and our elder care to understaffed facilities because we have no choice. There is less and less time for deep relationships, civic engagement, and community.

Civic Erosion: When you're exhausted and financially unstable, you don't volunteer for the fire department, you don't run for town council, and you don't have the emotional bandwidth to build connections. Civic participation, from voting to volunteering to simply knowing your neighbors, has declined sharply as economic insecurity has risen. The social fabric of a town wears thin.

We optimized the economy for labor market participation and GDP growth, and in the process, we de-optimized it for human happiness.

The Pillars Crumble

The collapse shows up in two places that are fundamental to a town's identity and its residents' sense of belonging: the homes and the main street.

The Vanishing Dream of Homeownership

A home is more than just a roof over your head. It used to be the primary way ordinary families built wealth, but also **stability, belonging, and a stake in the future**. It was a forced savings account, a source of pride, and an asset that represented a permanent place in the community. Today, that dream is dying. Young families can't save for a down payment while paying astronomical rent. Seniors can't find a smaller, affordable place to downsize into, so they stay in homes too big for them, blocking the natural cycle of housing.

The result is a generational lock-out from one of the core foundations of security. Without home equity, families can't weather emergencies, help their kids with college, or retire with dignity. Inequality becomes permanent, and the pathway to a stable, rooted life, is closed.

Walmart takes over

When I was very young, in the early 1980s, my siblings, cousins and I used to stay with my grandparents in Ohio every summer. They lived in a fairly prosperous working-class city, and one of the activities we would do to get out of the house was to go to the local five-and-dime, which was located in the downtown of their little city.

We would mainly window-shop, but occasionally my grandmother might buy us a little toy or trinket. Eventually, a Walmart moved into their area. At first, my grandparents were very excited that they could buy cheap products from a national chain. So in the summer we would get in the car, and instead of going to the five-and-dime, we would go to the Walmart.

About ten years after that, I was talking with my grandparents, and their downtown at that point had been completely emptied out, the five-and-dime long ago closed. There were very few shops left. The city, in an attempt to attract more people to downtown, had painted a series of murals on the wall that held back the Ohio River.

My grandfather lamented that it was like, "Putting a gold saddle on a dead horse." He went on to express regret that Walmart had moved to their city and had basically decimated the downtown.

The Hollowing of Main Street

The middle class wasn't just supported by big corporations, it was created and sustained by small businesses. The local diner, the independent hardware store, the family-owned pharmacy, these were community anchors. They provided good jobs, knew your name, and reinvested profits locally.

Now, they're being replaced by national chains and online giants. Since 1990, the share of retail spending going to small businesses has fallen by more than half. The profits don't circulate in town, they get vacuumed up to distant shareholders. Main Street empties out, and with it goes the town's unique character, its economic resilience, and its third places, the spots between work and home where community is formed. The same forces squeezing families are squeezing the small businesses that depend on them, creating a vicious cycle of communal decline.

The Ballast of Democracy

A disappearing middle class isn't just an economic problem. It's a direct threat to democracy and to societal happiness.

A broad, secure middle class has always been the ballast that keeps society stable and politics functional. When people have a tangible stake in the system and feel secure in their lives, they believe in it. They participate, they compromise, they plan for the long term. They have the emotional and financial security to engage as citizens.

When that security evaporates, society becomes unstable. Studies show that wider income inequality is strongly correlated with lower social trust, lower voter turnout, and higher political polarization. Distrust in institutions skyrockets. Political polarization becomes toxic because people aren't just arguing about ideas, they're fighting from a place of genuine fear, betrayal, and lost hope. Economic stagnation sets in because consumers have no money to spend on anything but survival.

Communities fragment because no one has the time or energy to hold them together.

We are living through the consequences of removing that ballast. We are witnessing the erosion of the very foundation upon which a happy, healthy, self-governing society is built.

Rebuilding the Middle Class

Restoring the middle class is the central task of our time. It's not about nostalgia for the 1950s. It's about creating a new, 21st-century stability where hard work is rewarded with security, where families aren't one crisis away from ruin, and where our towns have a future. It's about recognizing that a broad, secure middle class is not just an economic outcome, it is the social foundation for a nation dedicated to **the pursuit of happiness.**

A strong middle class was America's greatest innovation because it made that lofty promise a reality for millions. It can be our greatest renewal. But only if we choose to put first the people, and the communities where they build their lives.

Chapter 4: The Housing Crisis & The Path Home

I live in a 740-square-foot apartment above my old restaurant with my girlfriend and my son. I've been here since 2016. We want more kids, but in this space, that would be difficult. So for nine years, I've been searching for an affordable home within a reasonable drive of my business.

I remember the last house in my town that sold for under $300,000. It was around 2018.

When I served on the Town Council, another young councilor and I were both looking to buy houses. We brought it up to the other members. Their advice was a shrug: "You'll probably have to move north." There was no outrage or sense of crisis. Just acceptance that younger people could no longer afford to live in the communities they served.

Every year, I'd watch it happen: a regular customer, a recent college grad, a neighbor would stop coming in. They weren't leaving for a new job. They were moving to find a more affordable place to live. My friend who owns the café rents. My barber rents. My friend with the hair salon rents. None of us small business owners can afford to buy a home here.

This is the housing crisis, it is the single greatest determinant of your capacity to pursue **happiness**.

Housing dictates where you live, the size of your family, whether you can stay near aging parents, if you can build equity, and if your community has a future. A stable home is the launchpad for a flourishing life. Its absence is an anchor of perpetual anxiety. In New Hampshire, over 50,000 households are spending more than half their income on housing. This crisis was not an accident of the free market. It was built by design, and it directly undermines the foundational security our economy is supposed to provide.

The "Supply and Demand" Myth

Politicians love to say the housing crisis is simple: we need more supply. Just build! It's a comforting myth that sounds like economics.

Yes, we desperately need more homes. New Hampshire is short an estimated 30,000 housing units and that deficit is growing, but what kind of homes, where, and for whom? In New Hampshire, new construction overwhelmingly means large single-family homes or high-end apartments, units that generate maximum profit for developers, not stability for teachers, nurses, or retail workers.

In 2023, New Hampshire only permitted 4,878 housing units total, including just 1,773 units in buildings with 5 or more apartments; the kind that create density and affordability. The market, when left to its own devices in a distorted system, builds for capital returns, not for community need.

The real bottleneck isn't some abstract "free market." It's a thicket of government rules that strangle the market before it can function for the common good.

The Vicious Cycle:
When Raises Become Rent Increases

Here is the cruelest twist in the housing crisis. When you are struggling to pay rent, the obvious, moral solution seems to be higher wages. But in a housing market with a fixed supply, raising wages without building more homes is like adding more players to a game of musical chairs without adding more chairs.

I witnessed this in real-time during the pandemic. My employees started receiving rent increases from their landlords. I gave them raises to help cover the higher cost of housing. To pay for those raises, I had to raise the prices on my menu. One of our customers, my barber, Dan, got the same rent increase notice from his landlord. To cover it, he raised the price of a haircut. Everyone, now paying more for tacos and haircuts, had less disposable income. We all worked harder, and technically made more money on paper. But who ended up capturing most of that new money? The landlords.

Economists call this phenomenon rent capture. When the supply of a necessity like housing is artificially constrained, more money in renters' pockets does not create new apartments. Instead, it signals to property owners that the market can bear higher prices. The additional public support is partly transferred from tenants and taxpayers to landlords through higher rents. This is not a theory.

Research on federal housing vouchers finds that when voucher payment limits are made more generous across an entire metro area, landlords capture a meaningful share of the increase. They do this through higher rents in the voucher market, with only limited changes in unit quality or neighborhood quality. In other words, expanding assistance without rapidly expanding supply can inflate prices and dilute the intended benefit for families who need help most.

The lesson is stark: In a housing shortage, wage increases and **housing subsidies, by themselves, become rent increases.** We cannot solve this crisis by only focusing on paychecks. We have to fix the root cause: the severe shortage of homes.

My Intro to Zoning

My first introduction to zoning laws was the first day I sat on the Newmarket Zoning Board of Adjustment (ZBA). The ZBA is where a resident goes to request a variance to the rules around housing and development. The first case before us was a young man who wanted to build an apartment in his father's barn. His father was getting on in years, and he needed someone close by to take care of him.

It seemed reasonable to me. The town planner talked about how this type of Accessory Dwelling Unit (ADU) was a great way to help seniors "age in place." However, the zoning laws did not allow this ADU because the barn was not attached to the house. The other members of the board said, "Yes, we understand your need, but there is nothing we can do."

That made no sense to me. *Wasn't the point of having a board to intervene in cases like this?* I voted to allow him to build the apartment, but was outvoted by the other members of the board. The ironic thing to me, was that this guy could probably have gotten away with building the apartment in the barn without permission and no one would have noticed.

Origin of Zoning Laws

The idea of separating different types of buildings for public good is not new. The earliest modern zoning laws are traced to 18th century France, intended to keep polluting industries, slaughterhouses, and tanneries far from residential areas. It was a matter of public health.

But when this tool was imported to the United States, it was eventually twisted to serve a different, darker purpose: racial and economic segregation.

In the early 20th-century, American cities began using zoning not to separate factories from homes, but to separate people by race. The Supreme Court initially ignored this practice. However, in the 1917 case of *Buchanan v. Warley*, the Court struck down explicit racial zoning ordinances, ruling they violated the 14th Amendment.

This did not end the goal of segregation. It simply changed the method. The new tool was economic zoning.

The legal blueprint for modern exclusionary zoning was cemented in the 1926 Supreme Court case *Village of Euclid v. Ambler Realty Co.* While *Euclid* did not directly address race, it provided the perfect, race-neutral legal weapon. Cities and, later, suburbs could now mandate large lots, single-family homes, and expensive building materials. The effect was the same as an old racial covenant, it kept "undesirable" people out, but now the mechanism was income.

As housing historian Richard Rothstein wrote in his Spring 2021 *American Educator* article, "Suppressed History: The Intentional Segregation of America's Cities," local and federal officials promoted single-family zoning to "reserve middle class neighborhoods for single-family homes that lower income families of all races could not afford."

The intent to separate people by race was preserved, only the justification changed.

Zoning did not just shape our neighborhoods. It created artificial scarcity that drives our crisis. In many American cities, up to 75% of residential land is zoned so that it is legal to build only detached single-family homes. In New Hampshire, the zoning atlas finds that some towns zone 87% to 99.9% of their buildable acreage for small lot single-family housing. It is a government mandated shortage of the very homes that foster diverse, resilient, and integrated communities.

We now live in a world where a landlord can say to a tenant, "Due to market forces, I am raising your rent." Nothing has changed about the apartment. It did not get bigger or better, the only thing that changed is that demand for housing increased.

Yet this tenant cannot simply buy a plot of land, build an apartment building, and say, "The free market requires more housing, so I am building an apartment complex." In most areas of our state, that type of multi-unit property would not be allowed. So the "free market" is used to justify raising rents, but the same "free market" does not exist to build the housing necessary to lower them.

Now ask yourself a question: Who is sitting on the planning boards and zoning boards making these decisions? By and large, it is homeowners; people invested enough in the community to serve on a town board.

What incentive does a homeowner sitting on a land-use board have to increase housing? More housing could fundamentally hurt the value of their own home and, in the short term, offers them no real gain.

When we have public hearings to discuss potential new multifamily housing, often the people living in the neighborhoods where new housing is planned show up to object. The issue is, the potential renters who might benefit from this new housing typically do not show up to these hearings because they may not even live in that town yet. There is fundamentally no hypothetical tenant to be advocating for this new housing. The only person advocating for the building is the developer, who is frequently characterized as a greedy outsider.

Imagine if we treated other investments with the same restrictions we place on housing. Imagine if you wanted to buy a pickup truck and first had to ask all your neighbors for permission. Some might say, "I don't like pickup trucks. They cause too much pollution. I don't want to see an ugly pickup truck in my neighborhood. This is a neighborhood of minivans, it would be out of character to have a pickup parked here." That level of government control over what you do with your own property would never be tolerated. No one would stand for it. Yet these same types of arguments and controls are placed on housing, particularly the multifamily housing we desperately need to solve the housing crisis.

I strongly believe the founders of New Hampshire and the founders of these United States would never have allowed the planning and zoning laws we currently tolerate. They defy the very "Live Free or Die" ethos of New Hampshire.

My Intro to Zoning Continued…

Over the years I spoke to a number of residents who had been blocked from building apartments in their garages and barns because they were not attached to their houses. So when I eventually got elected to the Town Council I kept pushing to change the ADU ordinance.

Eventually, we had a public hearing. One of the residents who spoke against expanding ADUs said, "I'm concerned this could change the ***complexion*** of our town." I don't think he meant to be racist, but knowing what I did about the origin of zoning laws, I could not help but wonder *what exactly did he mean*? Another Town Councilor who did not support expanding ADU access said, "Imagine if we told the people on Maple Crest (a nearby residential neighborhood) that their neighbors were going to build an apartment next door…"

I didn't say it out loud, but all I could think was, "God forbid homeowners in our town have to live next to renters! Those renters might even be black or brown people. (Who are statistically more likely to rent.)" The unconscious classism and racism was palpable.

The reality is in New Hampshire, zoning and permitting rules often make affordable housing financially unworkable without government subsidy because they increase costs and delays while limiting the number of units that can be built.

The Forgotten History of Federally Built Housing

In an emergency, the U.S. government has repeatedly stepped in to construct housing directly. The most significant early example is the United States Housing Corporation (USHC). Created in 1918 during World War I, the USHC had a clear, urgent mission: to build quality homes for war workers flooding into industrial cities. In just over a year, it planned and partially constructed thousands of housing units in communities across the country. These were not barracks. They were well-designed neighborhoods with homes, schools, and community centers, built to a high standard with the belief that wartime workers deserved dignity.

For nearly half a century, the United States understood something we have forgotten today: housing is infrastructure. From the 1930s through the 1970s, the federal government invested directly in building homes for seniors, working families, and low-income households. These were not tax credits or speculative financial tools. These were real homes, constructed with public dollars, owned or operated by public or nonprofit partners, and offered at rents ordinary people could afford.

This era began with the 1937 Housing Act, which created the nation's public housing program. Federal dollars flowed to local housing authorities to build deeply subsidized homes intended to remain affordable over the long term. Contrary to the stereotypes that emerged later, many early public housing developments were solidly built and offered stability for working families.

As the population grew, federal housing programs expanded. Senior housing was added through Section 202 in 1959, allowing nonprofits to build very affordable homes for older Americans. Programs such as Section 221(d)(3) and Section 236 offered below market financing and mortgage subsidies to developers who agreed to maintain affordability. Together, these programs produced roughly 700,000 units nationwide and shaped the housing landscape for decades.

In 1974, Congress created Section 8, including a New Construction component that provided long term subsidies to build affordable apartment buildings. Over the next decade, project based Section 8 supported the development of hundreds of thousands of units, with production reaching the tens of thousands in many years. For a brief period, the United States had the capacity to produce affordable housing at national scale. Then, in 1983, Congress repealed the authority to enter into new Section 8 contracts tied to new construction and substantial rehabilitation, and the production system was effectively shut down.

The 1980s: When the Federal Government Stopped Building Houses

In the early 1980s, federal policy shifted away from building new subsidized homes. Housing and Urban Development commitments for federally financed units fell from 435,362 in 1976 to 60,590 by 1982, and Section 8 new construction and substantial rehabilitation were terminated in 1981. As a result, the national pipeline for new affordable housing shrank dramatically. Programs that built real, publicly accountable homes were replaced with complex tax credits for private developers. The goal shifted from creating homes for people to creating investment opportunities for capital. Affordability requirements became temporary. The pipeline of stable, foundational housing for working families dried up.

The federal government walked away and told the "market" to handle it. But the market, shaped by the exclusionary zoning we had created and a mandate to maximize shareholder profit, only builds what is most profitable, not what is most needed. We've been living with the consequences ever since: a national shortage of millions of homes. The U.S. is now short an estimated 3.8 million homes. We privatized the foundation of community and are shocked that it's now unaffordable.

The Consequences: A Community Unravels

The housing crisis doesn't just hurt individuals. It dismantles the ecosystems of stability within communities.

People delay having children or have fewer than they want. (I'm one of them.) Birth rates fall. New Hampshire's birth and fertility measures have fallen sharply since 1990, with the general fertility rate down about 27% and total births down about one third. The fundamental human joy and challenge of building a family is deferred.

For decades, the path to adulthood and community investment included a modest starter home: a small Cape, a duplex, a townhouse. It was the first rung on the ladder, where you built equity, stability, and ownership in the literal and figurative sense. You became a stakeholder in your block, your neighborhood, your town.

That rung on the ladder has been sawed off. Zoning laws across New Hampshire make it illegal to build these kinds of homes in most places. We've mandated large lots and single-family detached homes, which only developers of luxury properties can profitably build. The consequence is a generational lock-out.

Young adults stay in expensive rentals longer, unable to save a down payment. They delay marriage and children. Many simply leave the state, taking their energy, talent, and future spending with them.

Perhaps the most overlooked tragedy is what happens to our elders. Many own their homes outright but are cash-poor and house-rich. Rising property taxes and maintenance costs on a now-too-large house eat into fixed incomes. They'd love to downsize to a smaller, accessible apartment or condo in their own town, to stay near their doctor, their church, their friends, their life's memories. But those options often don't exist.

So they face a cruel choice: bleed their savings dry to stay in a home that no longer fits, or leave the community they helped build. In New Hampshire, nearly 32% of households with adults age 65 or older are housing-cost-burdened, paying more than 30% of income for housing.

Business Erosion

My restaurant suffered twice. I lost young customers who moved away. The customers who stayed had less to spend because their rent consumed nearly everything. A 2022 analysis highlighted by the Harvard Joint Center for Housing Studies found that lower income renters who spent more than 30% of their income on housing had about $600 a month left after paying rent and utilities. That $600 has to cover food, transportation, health care, child care, taxes, and the basic bills that keep life running, including insurance. That does not leave much room for anything extra, including a burger at my restaurant. A town where residents cannot afford to spend locally is a town where businesses cannot thrive. The cycle of community vitality is broken.

How We Engineered the Homelessness Crisis

America's homelessness crisis is not a natural disaster. For much of the twentieth century, there was an understanding that housing was a foundational need, and that when the market failed to provide it, the public had a role in increasing supply.

The turning point was the 1990s and programs like HOPE VI. Sold as a reform of distressed public housing, its stated goal was noble: replace concentrations of poverty with mixed-income communities. The diagnosis was correct: isolating extreme poverty undermines any neighborhood, but the prescription was often catastrophic. Nationwide, HOPE VI demolished about 98,592 public housing units. While new units were produced, only a little over half were replacement public housing, and many of the new homes served higher incomes than the families who had lived there before. Too often, the program functioned less as a rebuild and more as a retreat from public responsibility.

This change was fundamental. The federal government largely stopped building housing and instead relied on vouchers and market incentives. The theory was that private landlords would fill the gap. The reality is that a voucher is not a home. It is a coupon for a home that does not exist. In a housing shortage, vouchers cannot magically create new units. They push low-income renters into a brutal competition for the same scarce apartments.

The consequence is the crisis we live with. We transformed homelessness from a temporary emergency into a permanent condition. The system that once absorbed seniors on fixed incomes, people with disabilities, and families in temporary crisis was dismantled.

We now spend enormous sums managing the symptoms through shelters, motel placements, encampment enforcement, and crisis services. Meanwhile, a large body of evidence shows that for high need cases, permanent supportive housing can reduce costly use of shelters, jails, emergency rooms, and other crisis systems. We are paying for expensive temporary solutions instead of building homes.

The lesson of HOPE VI is not that mixed-income housing failed. It is that we abandoned the "building" part. Community First Economics demands we finish the job we walked away from: building mixed-income, publicly-funded housing at scale, treated as essential infrastructure. Homelessness is not inevitable. It is the direct, predictable outcome of engineered scarcity.

How the Housing Crisis Manufactures Division

One of the most corrosive effects of the housing crisis is not just economic, but social. It manufactures a scarcity mindset that pits neighbor against neighbor and turns community against newcomer.

When people are fighting for a secure, affordable home, they are living in a state of chronic anxiety. They see every new family as a competitor for a scarce resource: a roof over your head. This is not a moral failing of individuals. It is the logical, human reaction to a system of artificial scarcity.

Politicians and demagogues exploit this manufactured anxiety with lethal precision. They point to a strained shelter system or a crowded classroom and declare, "The problem is them. If we just kept them out, there would be enough for us." The rage should be aimed at exclusionary zoning, Wall Street landlords, and decades of federal disinvestment, and instead they blame immigrants, refugees, or anyone labeled an "outsider."

This is the ultimate political sleight of hand. It transforms a crisis of policy into a conflict between people.

The Community First solution dismantles this toxic logic. By treating housing as a foundational right and committing to build abundant, affordable homes for all who live and work here, we end the mindset of scarcity. When people feel secure in their own foundation, they are far more likely to extend a hand, not raise a fist.

The Vision: Connected Communities

Bad policy built this crisis. The escape route is built with better design for connection. Imagine neighborhoods with a humane mix of housing, the antithesis of exclusionary zoning:

Accessory Dwelling Units (ADUs or "granny flats"): behind existing homes, providing rental income for seniors or a first home for a young couple, while keeping extended families close.

Duplexes, triplexes, and townhomes: on single lots, creating more homes without changing the neighborhood's feel.

Small-scale apartment buildings: near main streets and transit.

Pocket neighborhoods: of cottages or congregate housing for seniors.

This kind of mixed-density, mixed-income, mixed-age neighborhood is how we knit the social fabric back together at the street level. It allows teachers, nurses, seniors, tradespeople, and young families to live near one another. Let's design neighborhoods to promote casual, daily interactions: on the sidewalk, at the corner store, in shared green spaces. Places where we build understanding, trust, and the spontaneous networks of mutual aid that define a true community.

The Tools: A Global & Local Toolkit

We don't need to invent solutions from scratch. We can look to places that have successfully treated housing as essential infrastructure.

The Vienna Model: Social Housing as the Standard

For over a century, Vienna has pursued a simple but radical idea: high quality, publicly supported housing should be normal, not a last resort. Today, about 43% of Viennese households live in subsidized housing, split between municipal housing and nonprofit or limited profit housing associations. These homes are not limited to the very poor.

They are available to a broad cross-section of residents, including teachers, nurses, students, and seniors. The system is built to keep housing costs moderate, often near a quarter of income, and recent research reports that Viennese households spent about 26% of their income on housing in 2022. It is a system that says the right to a stable home matters more than a developer's right to maximum profit.

The Cooperative Housing Model: Co-op City, New York

In the Bronx stands one of America's most successful large scale housing cooperatives: Co-op City, home to about 50,000 residents.

Residents buy shares in the cooperative corporation that owns the entire complex, which has more than 15,000 apartments. RiverBay Corporation is governed by an elected resident board, which means democratic control and stewardship focused on the long term. Built under New York's Mitchell-Lama Program, it offers an alternative to both the private rental market and traditional homeownership, a third option that puts community control first.

Singapore's Homeownership Model

In Singapore, about 77% of resident households live in public housing built by the Housing & Development Board. Most of these apartments are sold on 99 year leases, which allows households to build equity while keeping land under long term public control.

The government's land policies, including the Land Acquisition Act, made it possible to assemble land and plan entire new towns with schools, services, and transit. The result is a hybrid model: publicly planned and built, with widespread homeownership inside a regulated system. The core insight is that when homeownership is broad and attainable, people have more stability and more reason to invest in their communities.

Community Land Trusts (CLTs): An American Innovation

A nonprofit trust owns the land and leases it to homeowners, who own the building. When they sell, they get a fair return on their investment, but the resale price is capped, so the home stays affordable for the next working family. This breaks the speculative cycle and locks in affordability across generations.

In Burlington, Vermont, the Champlain Housing Trust owns and manages over 3,000 permanently affordable homes, including 684 shared equity homes. National research during the housing crash found that community land trust homeowners were about ten times less likely to be in foreclosure proceedings than homeowners in the conventional market.

Japan's Flexible Zoning

In Japan, zoning is national and relatively simple. The country uses 12 standardized land use zones, and most residential zones allow a range of housing types, from detached homes to small apartment buildings, by right. This legalizes much of the "missing middle" and lets neighborhoods adapt as demand changes.

In 2014, Tokyo permitted about 142,417 new homes, more than the entire state of California that year. Tokyo has not been immune to price cycles, but over long stretches its housing costs have generally been more stable than many peer global cities, helped by steady homebuilding.

A Community First Approach for New Hampshire

This vision requires specific, actionable policies. We can adapt proven models to fit New Hampshire.

Zoning reform: Build on the 2024 zoning reforms. Use incentives and model codes to legalize duplexes, triplexes, fourplexes, and small courtyard apartments in residential areas. Regulate for form, safety, and real community impacts, not for exclusion.

State funding for critical infrastructure: Many municipalities cannot add housing because they lack water, sewer, and wastewater capacity. Create dedicated state funding streams for these systems, with priority for projects that unlock mixed-income housing near existing town centers.

Statewide pre-approved ADU plan library: Following models like San José, partner with architects and code officials to publish a curated catalog of ADU designs that already meet building code requirements and local zoning standards. Homeowners choose a compliant design, approvals move faster, costs drop, and reform turns into real homes.

Launch cooperative housing initiatives: Provide technical assistance, seed funding, and favorable financing for resident owned housing cooperatives. Focus on converting existing apartment buildings when owners sell, and on developing new "missing middle" cooperatives that keep costs stable long term.

Invest in community land trusts: Provide robust state funding and technical support to expand community land trusts in every region, building a growing stock of homes that cannot be flipped to corporate landlords.

Build and train at the same time: Expand vocational school and correctional education programs that build modular homes, tiny homes, or components for affordable housing. Participation should be voluntary, wages should be real wages, and training should lead to recognized credentials and job placement. This builds housing, builds skills, supports reentry, and can reduce recidivism.

Unlock the existing stock with care: Offer low interest loans and grants that help homeowners add ADUs or convert underused space safely, including support for permitting, septic and sewer connections, and accessibility upgrades.

Create a New Hampshire Housing Corps: Establish a state level public developer, inspired by the United States Housing Corporation, to finance and build mixed-income, mixed generation housing on publicly owned land. The goal is permanently affordable, beautiful housing that is integrated into existing communities.

Expand New Hampshire Housing into a New Hampshire Housing Corps

The New Hampshire Business Finance Authority has shown that New Hampshire can use smart public finance tools to grow the economy while protecting taxpayers. Under state law, the BFA's total amount of state guarantees currently in place is capped at $200 million plus interest.

In practice, the BFA helps finance major facilities by purchasing or financing a building and leasing it back to the company with a path to ownership. For example, reporting on the SIG Sauer deal describes a structure where the BFA purchases a facility using bond financing and then leases it to SIG Sauer for ten years, with the company able to buy the property at the end of the term. A similar lease with an end of term purchase option has also been used for BAE Systems. (It should be noted that the BFA is focused on creating jobs regardless of the industry those jobs are in.)

So here is the obvious question. If we are willing to use this model to attract employers, why would we not use a similar model to build the housing those workers need in order to live here?

Our state already has the New Hampshire Housing Finance Authority. It finances affordable housing development, administers key tools like housing tax credits, and already operates a nonprofit predevelopment loan program.

What we do not have is a housing scale version of the BFA model that uses broad loan guarantees and credit enhancement to unlock private lending for the kinds of homes our communities actually need. The goal should be to build on New Hampshire Housing and expand its toolbox into a true Housing Corps, capable of financing housing at scale with the same seriousness that we finance economic development.

Housing as the Foundation for Society

Civilization began when humans began living together in huts. It was safer. It was more efficient. People could share labor, protect one another, raise children, and survive hard seasons. We are not solitary animals. We are built for cooperation.

When we fail to build enough homes, we are not just creating a market problem. We are breaking the basic conditions that make community possible. Forcing people back into tents, exposed to the elements, is a flashing warning sign that our system is not working. Many people worry that someday society might experience a collapse. For someone forced to live outside because there is no housing they can afford, society has already collapsed.

Housing is the primary physical platform for education, healthcare, family life, economic mobility, and social connection. Fixing housing is a prerequisite for rebuilding social trust, solidarity, and a truly welcoming community. You cannot build a "we" if everyone is desperately fighting for themselves.

A Community First housing policy asks a simple question: **What does a thriving human life require, from young adulthood to old age?** Then it builds the homes, the physical spaces, to make that life possible.

It's about restoring the cycle: making room for the next generation while honoring and keeping the last. It's about building towns where people feel a sense of belonging, at every age and stage. Where a young couple can imagine a future, a family can grow in stability, and an elder can be surrounded by a lifetime of connections.

That's the kind of community where the pursuit of happiness is a shared journey, not a solitary scramble. That's the only kind of community with a true future.

Chapter 5: The Property Tax & A Fair Funding System

My dad spent years complaining to me about property taxes. As a nuclear engineer, he saw the unfairness built into the math: wealthier towns paid a smaller share of their income for schools than poorer towns. I didn't fully grasp the implications until I bought my building in Newmarket.

In the early 2000s, our town faced a perfect storm. The old school was crumbling, filled with asbestos, the feds said we had to replace it. At around the same time, the EPA demanded a new water treatment plant. The state and federal governments offered little help. The bill landed squarely on us, the local taxpayers.

I supported the new school and the clean water. But forcing our little town to shoulder these massive costs alone felt like being punished for needing the basics. When my first tax bill arrived I owed over $6,000 for my 1,400-square-foot building! A decade earlier, I'd owned a 2,200-square-foot house just over the border in Maine. The taxes there were only $2,500.

That's when I understood my dad's criticism of the tax system. In New Hampshire, we attempt to fund the dream of equal opportunity with the most unequal tax imaginable, a tax that falls most heavily on the very communities that education is meant to uplift. **New Hampshire has one of the highest property tax burdens in the country. Property taxes are about 5% of personal income, compared with 3.1% nationally.**

But this is about more than fairness. It's about the pursuit of happiness. A tax system that demands a crippling share of a family's income for housing, threatens security, stability, and peace of mind, the essential precursors to a meaningful life. It taxes the foundation of community itself.

The Regressive Machine: A Tax on Stability

A "regressive" tax sounds like economic jargon. Here's what it means in human terms: it's a tax that takes a bigger slice from the income pie of the poor and middle class than from the rich.

Property taxes are regressive by nature; they aren't based on your income or your ability to pay. They're based on the assessed value of your home or business. A retired couple on a fixed pension in a modest home they've owned for 40 years can face the same crippling bill as a wealthy newcomer in a similar house. The tax doesn't care that one family's income is $40,000 and the other's is $400,000.

In New Hampshire, the poorest 20% of households pay about 6% of their income in property taxes, while the richest 1% pay about 2%. This creates a brutal irony. The very tax that funds our schools, the supposed engine of equal opportunity and future growth, guarantees that opportunity is distributed by zip code. It actively undermines the intergenerational promise that hard work and thrift will lead to security. Instead, it can turn a paid-off home, the embodiment of that promise, into a financial millstone for seniors.

Several years ago, I had a conversation with one of the customers at my restaurant who had bought his house in town in the 80s. He said, "I supported the new school. My kids went there, but I paid off my house several years ago and now my monthly property tax bill is the same as my mortgage payment used to be."

Schools Funded by Zip Code: The Geography of Opportunity

Here's the brutal math of New Hampshire's education funding, the system that shapes our children's futures:

•Roughly 70% comes from local property taxes.

•About 20% comes from the state.

•A mere 8-10% comes from the federal government.

New Hampshire has the lowest state share of education funding in America. This isn't a minor detail, it's the core of the crisis.

It means a town with a corporate park or luxurious lakefront homes can raise millions for its schools with a relatively low tax rate. A working-class town with modest homes must set a punishingly high tax rate just to afford the basics: new textbooks, a functioning heating system, a living wage for teachers.

The result is two separate worlds of childhood. In one, children have small classes, new technology, art programs, and well-supported teachers. In the other, they have leaking roofs, outdated books, constant budget cuts, and overcrowded classrooms. A child's educational foundation, and thus their capacity to learn, grow, and pursue their potential, is determined not by their innate talent or effort, but by their parents' property value. We have created a caste system based on real estate.

One of my friends is an art teacher in a town near the restaurant. One Friday night, she came in, sat at the bar, and ordered a margarita. I asked her how things were going at school. "It's hard," she said. "The school board keeps cutting funding to the arts department. I have to work on the weekends to pay my rent. I'm just exhausted. I love the kids, but I don't know how much longer I can keep doing this." My friend hadn't yet turned thirty, yet she was already burned out by the system.

Claremont: A Fight for the Future

In the 1990s, several New Hampshire towns, led by Claremont, had enough. They sued the state, arguing that this system violated the constitution. How could education be a fundamental right if its quality depended on a town's wealth?

The New Hampshire Supreme Court agreed. In a series of landmark rulings, it declared that the state has a constitutional duty to provide an "adequate" education for every child, and that relying on unequal local property taxes was illegal. The state, not individual towns, was responsible for fair funding. For a moment, there was hope. The state created the Statewide Education Property Tax (SWEPT) to pool money and redistribute it equitably.

But almost immediately, politics gutted the policy. Wealthy towns fought to keep "their" money, labeling themselves "donor towns" and arguing it was unfair to "donate" property tax revenue to less affluent communities. The legislature caved, allowing these towns to offset local revenue with their SWEPT contributions. Redistribution died.

The core flaw in the "donor town" argument is this: **any statewide tax will inevitably redistribute revenue from wealthier areas to those with greater need.** If we relied on an income tax, higher-earning cities would contribute more. If we turned to a sales tax, cities with more retail activity would contribute more into the system. That isn't unfair, it's the foundation of shared responsibility in a functioning society.

In New Hampshire, per pupil spending varies enormously across districts. In the latest statewide district data (FY 2023–2024), **the gap between the lowest and highest district cost per pupil is roughly $19,000 per student.** We won in court and lost in the statehouse. The promise of equal educational opportunity was deferred, again.

The Shell Game: "Low Taxes" as a Myth

Politicians boast about New Hampshire's "low taxes." But this is a shell game. We do not have a broad based sales tax or a broad based personal income tax, so we rely heavily on property taxes to pay for public services. New Hampshire is the most reliant state in the country on property taxes as a share of state and local revenue, which makes the burden especially heavy for many working and middle class households. We call it "local control," but every year more and more "locals" get priced out.

We've created a system where the wealthiest can live here, derive income from global investments, and pay almost nothing to the state that protects their assets and quality of life. At the same time a nurse or a factory worker pay a fortune just for the privilege of owning a modest home. That's not freedom. That's a rigged system.

The costs of this inequality are measured in more than dollars, they are measured in lost human potential and stolen futures:

Lost Potential: Study after study shows that students in well-funded schools are more likely to graduate, attend college, earn higher wages, and stay out of the criminal justice system. **A 10% increase in per-pupil spending leads to 7% higher earnings in adulthood.** Underfunding schools isn't saving money; it's stealing our future, depriving our state of innovators, caregivers, and informed citizens. It is a guarantee of future poverty, poor health, and overcrowded prisons.

The Senior Squeeze: Fixed-income seniors are literally taxed out of homes they've owned for a lifetime, breaking their ties to community, family, and the roots of their identity. We force a cruel choice between financial survival and belonging.

The Business Burden: As a small business owner, my property tax is a direct hit to my bottom line, it's a penalty for investing in a downtown building. It stifles the very local entrepreneurship and vibrant main streets that create communities worth living in.

By relying on the property tax as the backbone of local and school funding, we have turned the American Dream of **homeownership into a financial trap**. We encourage families to buy a home, the cornerstone of stability, then we tax them for it at rates that make it harder to save for their kids' education or their own retirement. We punish them for achieving the very security we claim to be "the American Dream".

Many years ago, I was listening to a call-in show on New Hampshire Public Radio. They were discussing property taxes. An older woman called in and said, "If it were up to me, we wouldn't let anyone move into our town who is under the age of 50. We just can't afford to keep paying for the kids' schools."

That really broke my heart.

What kind of state are we living in? We force communities to choose between funding decent education for young people or allowing elderly people on fixed incomes to stay in their homes. This is a Faustian bargain that is tearing our communities apart.

The Moral Case: Taxing Wealth, Not Work

Taxation is not theft. It is the membership dues we agree to pay to live in a functioning, prosperous, and just society. Every economy answers a simple, moral question: Who pays for civilization, and who benefits from it? Our roads, bridges, schools, courts, clean water, and safety nets are built and maintained with public resources, the pooled contributions of our shared enterprise.

The moral principle is simple: if you derive the greatest benefit from the system, you should pay the most to sustain it. This is about equity and reciprocity.

Community First Economics insists that fairness and sustainability must be the iron principles of taxation. A fair tax system doesn't punish success, but it ensures that those who have benefited most from our society contribute proportionally to its upkeep. It is the only way to lift the crushing, regressive burden off the middle and fund the shared foundations of community we all require.

The Community First Blueprint: Funding Fairness

Our goal is not to raise taxes for the sake of it. Our goal is to lower the overall tax burden on working and middle-class families by finally asking concentrated, often passive wealth to pay its way. The Claremont courts were right. Education is a right, not a privilege of geography. Community First Economics demands we finish the work they started.

Here is a practical, New Hampshire-focused blueprint to fund our communities fairly:

Fulfill Education Funding Promises with Sustainable Revenue & Bring Down Property Taxes: The core injustice is using a regressive property tax to fund the equal right to education. The state must meet its constitutional duty by creating a sustainable, fair revenue stream to fully fund the Education Trust Fund. The explicit goal must be to use this state money to dramatically bring down local property tax rates, providing direct, substantial relief to homeowners and renters.

Tax Speculation, Not Homes: Implement fees on non-owner-occupied, short-term rental properties that reduce the year-round housing stock, and dedicate the revenue to affordable housing trusts.

Reinstate and Modernize the Interest & Dividends Tax: From 1923 until 2021, New Hampshire had a 5% tax on interest and dividend income over a modest threshold. Its repeal was a massive gift to the wealthiest households, who derive the majority of their income from investments, not wages. **The New Hampshire Fiscal Policy Institute found that about 92% of the dollars from eliminating this tax stay with households in the top 20% of incomes, and slightly more than 58% of the benefit flows to the top 1%.** We should not only reinstate this tax but modernize it to better target passive, unearned income. This is the most straightforward, historically precedented way to ensure that wealth generated by capital assets contributes to the foundations it relies on.

Close Corporate Loopholes & Establish a Minimum Corporate Tax: Profitable corporations doing business in New Hampshire should pay a minimum effective tax rate. If you benefit from our market, our workforce, and our infrastructure, you must pay to maintain them.

Consider Walmart and Amazon, two of the largest retailers operating in our state. Walmart runs more than 25 stores and a major distribution center here. Amazon operates fulfillment centers, delivery stations, and Whole Foods locations. Both generate billions in sales to New Hampshire residents and depend on our roads, utilities, public safety, and educated workforce. Yet through legal loopholes, interstate profit-shifting, and strategic deductions, these corporate giants often pay far less in state business taxes than a Main Street shop with a fraction of their revenue.

We can fix this without imposing a sales tax on consumers. Here's how:

Enact a Corporate Minimum Tax Based on New Hampshire Sales: If a corporation's standard Business Profits Tax or Business Enterprise Tax liability falls below a threshold tied to its in-state sales, they pay a minimum tax based on those sales instead. For example, a 0.5% minimum tax on in-state gross receipts over $100 million would ensure that large, profitable corporations contribute meaningfully;

even if deductions zero out their reported profits.

Expand the Business Enterprise Tax with a Large Retailer Surcharge: Amend the BET to include a small additional percentage on the gross receipts of corporations with New Hampshire sales exceeding $100 million. This would apply only to the largest players and not local businesses. This would function as a fee for the privilege of accessing our market at scale.

Apply a Marketplace Facilitator Fee on Digital Sales: For companies like Amazon that act as platforms for third-party sales, impose a small fee on gross sales facilitated in New Hampshire. This recognizes the value these corporations extract from our economy and ensures they help maintain the infrastructure that makes their business model possible.

These approaches are not sales taxes.

We don't need to reinvent the wheel. States like Massachusetts, Oregon, and California already use gross receipts thresholds or corporate minimum taxes to ensure large corporations can't shift profits and avoid paying into the systems they rely on. It's time New Hampshire did the same.

A fair tax system doesn't punish success, it rewards responsibility. And it ensures that our schools, roads, and communities are funded by those who use them most.

The Choice: Investment vs. Extraction

The revenue from this fairer system is not an end in itself. It is an investment with a massive public return in security, opportunity, and community vitality. More importantly, it secures our fiscal future against the coming waves of economic change.

Why a wealth focus is future-proof: The AI and automation revolution will mean fewer people earning traditional wages. Relying on income and sales taxes will mean a collapsing revenue base just as we need more resources for transition, retraining, and social support. Taxes on investment income, capital gains, and corporate profits ensure that the wealth generated by technology and capital assets contributes to the society that makes them possible. New Hampshire's old Interest and Dividends tax was a start. We need to finish the job and build a system worthy of a 21st-century economy.

This is the choice before us. We can cling to the myths of the past and to a tax system built for a 20th-century economy of factories and wages. Or we can be bold and build a 21st-century tax system for a Community First future: one that taxes the idle wealth of the past to build the shared prosperity and security of the future.

A fair tax system is our community's scorecard. It shows that we value broad-based growth, opportunity, and long-term renewal over concentrated wealth, exclusion or short-term extraction.

We are not a poor state or a poor country. We have the resources.

We can choose differently. We can choose to fund our common future fairly, so that every child in New Hampshire, from Colebrook to Conway to Claremont, has the same solid education foundation to build upon.

Property Taxes: Limiting Economic Growth

When I first opened Jonny Boston's International in Newmarket, the building's antique charm was obvious. A granite stone building built in 1835, it stood long before anyone imagined a world of cars. The locals were skeptical. "It's never gonna work out," they'd say. "That spot's got no parking."

In the beginning, we made it work. Customers found spots where they could, walked a little farther, and made it part of the routine. When I finally bought the building in 2016, I thought maybe I could help fix the problem for everyone downtown. I got involved, joined the Zoning Board, and later, on the Town Council, I helped start a parking committee. We had plans. We had studies. The need was clear.

What we didn't have was the money.

That's when I ran headlong into the math of New Hampshire. Our town was pouring everything it had into our schools, funded almost entirely by our local property taxes. There was nothing left. No two million dollars for a simple parking garage, the kind of thing that would help my business and every other shop on Main Street, was out of reach. The growth of my business wasn't limited by my ideas or our customers. It was limited by the tax system.

I'd have a good year at the restaurant. We'd be busy, the community showed up, the numbers looked good. Then the property tax bill would land. Over six thousand dollars for our small space. That feeling of momentum, of getting ahead, would just drain away. It was like shoveling water. No matter how hard we worked, a huge piece of whatever we earned went right back out the door. Not to a supplier, not to an employee, but to a tax bill.

That's when it stopped being a policy debate and started being my life. The issues in this book, such as property taxes, school funding, and why our towns feel stuck, weren't ideas I read about in the news. They were the wall I kept hitting. I realized I couldn't just be a business owner who grumbled about taxes. If I wanted to build a future here, for myself and for this town, I had to try to change the system.

That's why I first ran for Governor in 2024. I saw that the future in New Hampshire would continue to get worse for people like me and for working families, small business owners and retirees. We had to tackle one big, tangled mess. We had to fix housing. We had to fund our schools in a way that made sense. And we had to stop crushing people with property taxes. You can't solve one without solving the others.

This book is my attempt to map a way out. It's about how we build the parking, fund the school, and keep the businesses' doors open as one shared project. It's about remembering that our economy is just the management of our home, and doing it in a way that lets everyone in the house survive.

Chapter 6: The Myth of the Self-Made Millionaire & The Rise of the Corporation

"I believe that we shouldn't be settling for crumbs while billionaires eat the cookie we baked." – Graham Platner

The Myth: The Hidden Public Platform

We often hear the argument that wealthy people are the "job creators," and that taxing them hurts everyone else. It's the moral cornerstone of trickle-down economics: their success is our success, and their wealth is a sign of virtue. We're told they "built that," and thus owe nothing to society.

Having run a small business, I've learned this is a fantasy and a **dangerous fiction**. The truth is the opposite: *the wealthy rely on the government, and by extension, on all of us, far more than the middle class or the poor.* Their fortunes are not built in a vacuum. They are harvested from a field we all plowed, planted, and watered together. That's precisely why they have the greatest responsibility to reinvest in the soil.

This myth is a poison in our politics and our community spirit. It justifies inequality, erodes our sense of shared destiny, and corrodes the reciprocal obligations that make a society function. It denies the fundamental truth that all individual pursuit of happiness depends on a massive, shared, publicly-built foundation.

The Hidden Subsidy of Wealth: The Invisible Platform

We call these things "public goods," but let's be blunt: they are wealth multipliers. They are the infrastructure that turns a good idea into a global fortune, a garage startup into a household name.

Think about any modern fortune. Jeff Bezos's empire depends on a web of public investments he didn't build. Packages from China move on seas protected by the U.S. Navy. They travel on highways built and maintained by taxpayers. They are delivered to doors in neighborhoods kept safe by police and fire departments, via an addressing system created by the postal service. Bezos's contracts are enforced by public courts. His entire online marketplace depends on the internet, a technology born from government research and defense spending.

The internet's foundational technologies such as ARPANET and the World Wide Web, were funded by U.S. taxpayers through DARPA, the NSF, and CERN. Private enterprise commercialized what the public pioneered.

Bezos and his fellow billionaires aren't standing alone on a mountaintop of their own making. They're standing on a massive, publicly-funded platform. And the myth of the "self-made" individual encourages them, and us, to pretend that platform isn't there, so they can justify pulling the ladder up after themselves.

Let's itemize the public platform every fortune rests upon:

The Public Works of Commerce: Roads, bridges, ports, the electric grid, the air traffic system, satellites for GPS. The U.S. highway system alone was built at a public cost of over $500 billion (in today's dollars) and enabled an estimated 11 billion tons of freight in 2024.

The Rule of Law: The entire concept of enforceable contracts, stable currency, protected property rights, and patent law is a government service. Without it, there is no "Fortune 500," only chaos and force.

The Educated Workforce: Every employee is trained by a public K-12 system. Every breakthrough in tech, medicine, or engineering rests on basic science from public universities and government grants. Roughly 73% of all science papers cited on the front page of U.S. industry patents had origins in publicly funded research.

The Innovations They Inherit: The internet, GPS, touchscreens, and countless medical advances were seeded by government grants and military research. The private sector brilliantly refined and monetized what the public sector pioneered and de-risked.

The irony is breathtaking. Those who benefit most from this collective investment are often the loudest in denouncing "government" and their duty to sustain it. But strip away the public platform, and their fortunes, and our collective capacity for innovation and security, collapse.

Corporate Transformation: From Public Tool to Private Power

"I hope we shall crush in its birth the aristocracy of our monied corporations which dare already to challenge our government to a trial of strength." – Thomas Jefferson

How did we get here? How did an entity meant to serve the public good become a power over it? The story of the corporation holds the answer.

The Public Tool (1700s - Early 1800s)

In the early days of New Hampshire and the republic, a corporation was nothing like today's multinational entity. It was a public franchise, created by a specific act of the state legislature for a narrow, public purpose.

A charter might authorize a company to build a bridge, dig a canal, or operate a mill. These charters came with strict limits: what the corporation could do, how long it could exist, what it could charge, and often, a requirement that it revert to public ownership after a set period. The logic was straightforward and grounded in the common good: a corporation drew its right to exist from the community, and therefore had to serve the community. It was a means to a public end, a tool for building a shared foundation of prosperity.

This concept was so ingrained that when the founders revolted against Britain, a corporate entity was one of their prime targets. In 1773, the Boston Tea Party was a protest against a tax. It was also against a corporate bailout. The British government had granted the East India Company a monopoly on tea imports and a tax break, threatening to crush colonial merchants. The revolutionaries saw this clearly: a government using its power to enrich a connected corporation at the public's expense. Their pursuit of happiness required freedom from such unaccountable, profit-driven power.

The Legal Transformation: Dartmouth College v. Woodward (1819)

New Hampshire sits at the center of the pivotal moment when this public tool began to morph into a private power. In 1816, our state legislature tried to reorganize Dartmouth College, a private corporation. The college resisted, claiming its royal charter was a contract. The case reached the U.S. Supreme Court.

In 1819, in *Dartmouth College v. Woodward*, the Court ruled in the college's favor. A corporate charter was a contract, protected by the Constitution, and could not be altered by the state. This decision was a seismic shift. It began the process of transforming the corporation from a public instrument into a private, autonomous entity with legal rights akin to an individual; rights without the commensurate responsibilities of citizenship.

Over the next century, through a series of court cases and laws, corporations gained more of these "personhood" rights. Yet, as legal scholar Justice John Paul Stevens later noted in his *Citizens United* dissent, they "have no consciences, no beliefs, no feelings, no thoughts, no desires" like real human beings. Their one overriding legal duty, as would soon be cemented, is to maximize shareholder profit. The purpose was narrowing from public benefit to private gain.

The Legal Lock-In: The Profit Mandate

A single courtroom battle in Michigan in 1919 would lock shareholder power into law and redefine the very purpose of the American corporation for the next century. It's the story of Henry Ford and his own shareholders, the Dodge brothers.

In 1914, Henry Ford's Model T was a smash hit. The Ford Motor Company was rolling in cash; Ford made a startling announcement. He would slash the price of the Model T yet again, and, most radically, he would more than double his workers' daily pay to the famous $5-a-day wage.

His reasoning was visionary. He argued that well-paid workers would become loyal customers, that reducing turnover would save costs, and that a prosperous working class was essential for a stable, growing economy. He famously said the company should make *only a reasonable profit* and that the rest belonged *in some way to the public*. He saw his corporation as part of a social ecosystem that enabled widespread economic benefits.

But two of his largest shareholders, John and Horace Dodge, were furious. They sued Ford, demanding he stop his expansion plans and distribute the massive profits as dividends.

The case, *Dodge v. Ford Motor Company (1919)*, reached the Michigan Supreme Court. The court's decision was a thunderclap that still echoes in every corporate boardroom today.

The court ruled against Henry Ford.

In its landmark opinion, the court declared:

A business corporation is organized and carried on primarily for the profit of the stockholders.

Ford's desire to benefit his workers and the public was, in the eyes of the law, a dereliction of duty. The corporation, the court decreed, existed for one supreme purpose: to maximize shareholder value.

This was the final, legal severing of the corporation from any inherent public purpose. No longer a franchise granted for communal benefit, it was now a private financial vehicle. The "community" in its calculus was reduced to a cost center: wages to be minimized, taxes to be avoided, regulations to be resisted. This was all done in the service of that quarterly dividend. The legal mandate to contribute to a sustainable community was replaced by a mandate to extract value from them.

When Taxes Forced Investment

The 1950s is considered by many as the golden age of American prosperity. This was an era when a single income supported a family, when workers could expect steady pay raises, and the government invested in public infrastructure. But these investments that built the middle-class did not happen by accident.

In this post World War II era, the top marginal corporate tax rate hovered around **52%**. For every dollar of profit above a high threshold, more than fifty cents went to the federal government. This created a powerful, simple incentive: if you couldn't keep the money, what was the smartest thing to do with it?

Corporations were faced with a choice: they could write a check to the U.S. Treasury, or they could reinvest that capital in ways that were deductible, deferred, or simply smarter for long-term growth. This tax code channeled success. It made spending on innovation, worker training, and higher wages the rational business decision.

Research & Development boomed, because investing in tomorrow's products was better than taxing today's profits.

Capital investment soared, as companies built new factories and upgraded equipment instead of surrendering earnings.

Wages rose, because putting money into the pockets of loyal, skilled workers through salaries, pensions, and benefits, built a more stable and productive company.

This was the hidden engine of mid-century prosperity. The high tax rate wasn't a penalty, it was a structural nudge. It told capital: *If you want to retain value, you must create value for your community.* Profits were recycled into the foundations of shared prosperity.

The contrast with today is stark. After decades of rate cuts, the corporate tax burden has plummeted. The incentive has flipped. Now, the most rational way to retain value is often to extract it. Corporations achieve this through stock buybacks, dividend payments, and financial engineering that boosts share price in the short term. The money that once flowed into factory floors and worker paychecks now flows to shareholder accounts, often untaxed at the corporate level and lightly taxed as capital gains.

We changed the question from "**How do we build something lasting?**" to "**How do we extract value quickly?**" The high tax rates of the 1950s didn't stifle the American economy; they disciplined it toward productive, long-term investment. They forced capital to build, not just harvest.

Community First Economics understands this lesson: tax policy is not just about raising revenue. It is a blueprint. It tells capital where to go. In the 1950s, the blueprint said: *Invest here, in the real economy*. We need a new blueprint that says the same thing.

The Pathology of Extraction: From Obsolescence to Consumerism

If *Dodge v. Ford* provided the legal command to prioritize profit above all, then the strategies of Planned Obsolescence became the practical execution of that command, directly attacking the ecological sustainability of capitalism.

The Phoebus Cartel (1924): The Blueprint for Failure

In 1924, the world's leading light bulb manufacturers, including General Electric, Philips, and Osram, formed the Phoebus cartel. Their agreement created a universal standard: bulbs would last 1,000 hours.

Earlier bulbs could last 2,500 hours or more. The cartel's engineers didn't improve longevity, instead they chose to shorten it. Manufacturers whose bulbs exceeded the limit were fined. The cartel justified this standard in the language of efficiency, brightness, and compatibility; reasonable goals for a growing global market. But the result was the same: a dramatically shorter product life that turned light bulbs from durable goods into recurring purchases. The proof lies in the results of their collusion, not in their stated goal.

The now-famous Centennial Light Bulb in Livermore, California, burning since 1901, shows that much longer life was technically possible, even if dimmer or less efficient.

By standardizing obsolescence, Phoebus shifted power from the consumer who wanted a lasting product to the corporation that needed perpetual sales. It was a business model that wasn't built on improving quality, but on ensuring its decline. This was a blueprint that would shape entire industries for the next century.

Manufacturing a Culture of Waste: The 1956 Plastics Conference

If Phoebus attacked product durability, the plastics industry of the 1950s set out to attack the public's mentality. In the post-war boom, chemical companies faced a problem: a massive surplus of production capacity from the war effort. Their solution, unveiled at the now-infamous 1956 National Plastics Conference, was to convince the public that throwing things away was modern and virtuous.

Lloyd Stouffer, the editor of *Modern Packaging* magazine, delivered the conference's keynote with chilling clarity. **"The future of plastics is in the trash can,"** he declared. He urged manufacturers to start seeing packaging as a single-use, instantly disposable sales tool. The explicit goal was to actively shift the public psyche from the ethic of reuse and thrift, the mindset that weathered the Depression and won the war, to one of convenience and waste.

This was a coordinated, industry-wide campaign. Single-serving packages, plastic bags, and disposable cups were marketed as liberating. When public concern about plastic waste grew in the 1960s, the industry pioneered blaming the consumer. The famous "Crying Indian" ads of the "Keep America Beautiful" campaign (funded by beverage and packaging companies) framed pollution as a problem of individual littering, not of systemic overproduction. Later, they championed recycling as a catch-all solution, despite knowing most plastics were never economically recyclable. **Less than 9% of plastic produced is recycled in the U.S. today.** The point of the recycling symbol was to pacify consumer guilt and stave off laws that would limit production. It made trash our moral failing when it should have been their engineering goal to design a sustainable product.

Consumerism as the New Civic Religion
"There is a God-shaped vacuum in the heart of each man which cannot be satisfied by any created thing..."
– Blaise Pascal

The story of Phoebus and the Plastics Conference reveals something deeper than just business strategy. It shows the birth of a new civic religion for America: Consumerism.

For centuries, communities were bound together by shared values: thrift, craftsmanship, neighborliness, saving for hard times, and stewardship of resources that would be passed to the next generation. These were communal survival strategies that built trust and resilience. In New England this was called "Yankee ingenuity."

The 20th-century corporations systematically dismantled this old faith and replaced it with a new one. In their new gospel:

•Salvation comes through purchase (not through character or

community)

•Identity is expressed through brand loyalty (not through craft, skill, or place)

•Progress is measured in newness and disposability (not in durability and repair)

•The good life is defined by what you own (not by who you are or how you contribute)

Advertising spending in the U.S. grew from $6 billion annually in 1950 to over $300 billion today, a 50-fold increase. Advertising became the priesthood of this new religion. The shopping mall replaced the town square as the cathedral of community life. Black Friday became a high holy day. This was cultural engineering on a massive scale. It was a deliberate rewiring of the American psyche to serve corporate profits.

The "Right to Repair" movement is, at its heart, a heresy against this consumerist religion. It asserts that stewardship, skill, and thrift are moral goods. It says that our relationship with objects should be one of care and longevity, not disposable consumption. It rejects the doctrine that newer is always better. When a farmer cannot fix his own tractor due to software locks, or you cannot replace your iPhone battery, it is the legal enforcement of obsolescence. It criminalizes Yankee ingenuity.

The Pathology of Wealth: When Accumulation Becomes Illness

Beyond the economic arguments lies a psychological fact supported by both primate research and modern psychology: extreme, compulsive wealth accumulation is not rational economic behavior. It is often dysfunctional behavior that harms both the accumulator and the community.

In Yale's famous "monkey capitalism" experiments, researchers gave capuchin monkeys tokens to trade for food. The monkeys quickly developed what looked like human economic pathologies: some hoarded tokens long after their needs were met, others engaged in high-risk "gambling" for more, and social hierarchies formed around token wealth. The primates' behavior wasn't optimizing for survival or well-being; it was pursuing accumulation for its own sake, disrupting social bonds in the process.

Modern psychology observes similar patterns in humans under terms like "wealth addiction" or *plutomania*. When accumulation becomes compulsive and continues despite damaged relationships, personal isolation, and harm to the community. This behavior mirrors the clinical patterns of addiction: reduced tolerance (needing more to feel secure), withdrawal (anxiety when wealth fluctuates), and continuation despite clear negative consequences.

This isn't about diagnosing individuals. It's about recognizing a socially pathological pattern that our current economic system not only permits but celebrates. *Dodge v. Ford* legally enshrines what might otherwise be seen as disordered behavior: the compulsive pursuit of profit above all other human considerations. The corporations put profit over health, community, environment, and even the long-term viability of the corporation itself.

The wealthiest 1% of Americans now own more wealth than the entire middle class. The billionaire who accumulates more wealth than could be spent in a thousand lifetimes, while fighting to pay less in taxes that fund the schools and roads his business depends on, is not exhibiting economic rationality. He is exhibiting a failure of **economic and social rationality.** This is a disconnect from the reality that his fortune depends on the very foundations he undermines.

This pathology has ancient roots. The Greeks called it *pleonexia:* the insatiable desire for more than one's fair share, which they considered a vice that destroyed both the individual and the *polis*. Modern economics calls it "maximizing utility." But when the "utility" being maximized is abstract digits in a bank account, at the cost of sustainable human growth, we must ask: What, exactly, are we **optimizing for?**

Community First Economics offers a healthier model: one that recognizes that economic success shouldn't be measured in hoarded capital, but in community well-being. It realigns our economic system with human psychology's deeper need: not for endless accumulation, but for connection, purpose, and legacy.

A Broken Social Contract

As wealth concentrates, the wealthy don't use their power to become less dependent on the system. They use it to capture it, to bend the rules for their own benefit, socializing risk and privatizing reward. This is where the myth turns actively destructive.

Tax Loopholes & Offshoring: They lobby for lower rates, offshore havens, and "carried interest" rules, ensuring the effective tax rate for billionaires is often lower than for their secretaries. The 400 wealthiest American families paid an average federal income tax rate of just 8.2% in recent years; lower than that of a teacher or firefighter. They benefit from the system, then lobby to defund it.

Corporate Welfare: Entire industries such as fossil fuels, agribusiness, Wall Street, survive on subsidies, bailouts, and sweetheart deals, all defended by armies of lobbyists. The U.S. federal government spends an estimated $181 billion annually on corporate subsidies. We're told it's a "free market," but it's rigged enterprise.

Regulatory Capture: They fund the campaigns of the officials meant to regulate them, ensuring rules protect incumbents, stifle competition, and externalize costs (like pollution) onto the public.

This isn't free enterprise. It's a betrayal of the social contract. The true working class subsidizes the wealthy twice: first through their taxes that build the platform, and second through policies that redirect public wealth upward and undermine our shared foundation.

History's Warning

This imbalance is not stable. History shows a clear lesson: when too much wealth and power concentrate at the top, societies fracture, often violently. The greed of the few destroys the possibility of happiness for the many, leading to upheaval.

Ancient Rome: The Republic disintegrated as land and wealth pooled among a senatorial elite. Attempts at reform were met with assassination, foreshadowing a century of civil war.

France, 1789: A nobility exempt from taxes bled the peasantry dry. The monarchy's failure to reform led to revolution and terror.

America, 1929: The Roaring Twenties enriched speculators while workers' wages stagnated. The resulting Great Depression sparked the

New Deal, a **peaceful revolution** that rebalanced capitalism through regulation, social security, and progressive taxation. It was a course correction that saved capitalism from itself by reaffirming the public foundation.

The pattern is unmistakable. Societies that refuse to correct extreme inequality and rebuild the social contract through reform eventually correct it through chaos. The elite have a choice: *share through policy and invest in the common foundation, or risk losing everything when the foundation crumbles.*

America at the Tipping Point

Today, the United States faces inequality rivaling the Gilded Age. The top 0.1% own more wealth than the bottom 80% combined. In a nation founded on the promise of opportunity, this is more than just an economic statistic. It is a warning. Unchecked wealth inequality destroys **democracy.** Political power follows money. When wealth is this concentrated, policy follows the donor class, not the people. The result is the political numbness, rage, and lost faith we see all around us, a direct threat to our collective pursuit of a decent society.

As Franklin D. Roosevelt warned in 1936, battling the "economic royalists" of his day:

"We know now that Government by organized money is just

as dangerous as Government by organized mob."

He saved capitalism by reforming it. He understood that **taxing the rich is the price of stability, and investment in the common foundation is the price of lasting prosperity and peace.**

The choice before our generation is the same as in Rome, France, and 1929 America. We can choose to rebuild a system of shared prosperity, reciprocal obligation, and lasting peace by investing in our common foundation. Or we can cling to the myth, until the whole crumbling structure comes down around us.

Community First Economics is an invitation to choose wisely. To remember that we're all in this together.

Community First Reform

The goal is not to abolish the corporation. It is to restore it to its proper role within a society dedicated to life, liberty, and the pursuit of happiness: a powerful tool for enterprise that operates within a framework of community obligation and contributes to the foundations of widespread economic growth.

This requires a new charter, a new social contract for the 21st century:

Conditional Privileges on Community Value: Corporate benefits (tax breaks, permits, limited liability) must be tied to demonstrable community value: good jobs, local investment, environmental stewardship.

Enforce Extended Producer Responsibility (EPR): The polluter must pay. If a company sells a product in New Hampshire, it is financially responsible for its entire lifecycle: collection, recycling, or safe disposal. This aligns the profit motive with the long-term health of our communities and environment.

Enshrine a Strong "Right to Repair": Pass laws guaranteeing owners and independent shops access to parts, tools, and software. This supports local small businesses, empowers individuals, and pushes back against the engineered waste that fuels the linear economy.

Support the True Engines of Community Happiness: Use policy to actively favor small, local, worker-owned, and cooperative businesses. These types of enterprises keep profits circulating locally and are accountable to people, not distant shareholders.

The Mondragon Corporation: in Spain, is the world's largest cooperative. Founded in a postwar region of poverty, it now employs over 80,000 worker-owners in manufacturing, finance, retail, and education. Profits are shared equitably, executive pay is capped, and wealth stays rooted in the community. Mondragon funds schools, supports local suppliers, and proves that large-scale enterprise can thrive while being democratic, accountable, and deeply human.

New Hampshire has its own proud co-op tradition. By nurturing worker-owned businesses in housing, clean energy, and manufacturing, we can build an economy where success is shared, stability is baked in, and the growth of the community is a collective endeavor.

Society once understood that the corporation was our creation. We gave it life to serve us, to help build the common foundations for our pursuit of happiness. We have the power, as voters, as citizens, as a state legislature, to rewrite the rules.

The rise of the corporation was not inevitable. It was a series of choices. We can make new ones. We can build an economy where corporations are strong parts of our communities, not powers over them. It begins by remembering a simple fact: We the people grant the corporate charter. We the people can demand it serve the public good and contribute to the foundations of a society where mutual assured happiness is the goal.

Chapter 7: The Price of Democracy

When I was four or five years old, I learned about John F. Kennedy and told my mother I wanted to be President someday. She laughed and said, "I hope you're rich, because only rich people get to be President."

As a child, I was confused and didn't want to believe her. I've spent much of my life waiting to see her proven wrong, to know that democracy is real, and that anyone can serve. But the older I got, and the closer I look, the more I see my mother's depressing honesty. We have built a system where money doesn't just influence politics, it selects the politicians. It drafts the legislation. It sets the agenda.

This is the final, fatal symptom of the disease. When economic inequality reaches a boiling point and when wealth concentrates into the hands of a few, government is reduced to auctioning off the levers of power. It makes a mockery of "one person, one vote" and transforms the grand, collective project of self-government into a private bidding war.

Citizens United: The Legal Earthquake

In 2010, the Supreme Court's *Citizens United v. FEC* decision drastically changed the nature of American citizenship. By ruling that corporations could spend unlimited sums on elections, equating money with "speech," the Court handed a megaphone to the wealthiest individuals and largest corporations. In a crowded town square of public debate, it gave a whisper to most citizens and a deafening roar to a select few.

The floodgates opened. So-called "Super PACs" and dark money networks, where donors can be hidden, now spend billions every election cycle. In the 2020 federal elections, outside spending by Super PACs and other groups exceeded $3.2 billion, more than triple the amount spent in 2010. In the 2024 elections, Super PACs raised over **$4.29 billion and spent $2.73 billion**, part of an overall surge in outside spending that continues to reshape federal campaigns. As Senator Dick Durbin would later say, "The Supreme Court has given the green light to a new system of writing large checks in return for political access and influence."

This legal shift created a new political physics: influence is proportional to donations. If you cannot afford to buy a megaphone, you are functionally silent on the issues that shape your life, your family's security, and your community's future. The democratic process, meant to be our shared tool for negotiating our common life and building foundations for happiness, was corrupted at its core.

The Golden Rule: He Who Has the Gold Makes the Rules

Wealthy donors and corporate lobbies don't spend billions on political campaigns for fun. They do it for a return on investment. Their policy preferences are translated into law with chilling efficiency, often against overwhelming public opinion.

Consider tax policy. The consistent, decades-long drive to cut taxes for the wealthy and corporations continues, even in the face of massive public opposition. In 2023, 66% of Americans said corporations pay too little in taxes, and 65% said the wealthy pay too little. Yet, the Tax Cuts and Jobs Act of 2017 slashed the corporate tax rate from 35% to 21%, delivering an estimated $1.3 trillion windfall to corporations and the top 1%. It is a direct translation of donor priorities into law.

Or look at the stalled fight against climate change. Legislation fails under the weight of fossil fuel lobbying, despite clear scientific urgency, sacrificing our shared environment for quarterly profits. The fossil fuel industry spent over $2.4 billion on federal lobbying from 2000 to 2023, while renewable energy spent less than one-tenth that amount.

Perhaps the clearest example is cannabis legalization. For over a decade, national polls have consistently shown support from two-thirds of Americans, including majorities of Democrats, Republicans, and Independents. The public will is unambiguous. Yet, at the federal level, it remains a Schedule I drug alongside heroin. Why? Follow the money. The alcohol, pharmaceutical, and tobacco industries, along with the private prison and prison guard unions that profit from incarceration, spend millions on lobbying to maintain prohibition. So, despite overwhelming public consensus, a well-funded coalition of special interests can veto the people's will.

Study after study confirms this shocking disconnect. Political scientists Martin Gilens and Benjamin Page analyzed decades of policy decisions and concluded: **"The preferences of the average American appear to have only a minuscule, near-zero, statistically non-significant impact upon public policy."** Major economic elites and organized interest groups, however, have substantial influence.

In other words, if you're not a major donor, you're not a constituent in the eyes of the system. You're part of the audience. The elites have manipulated the goal of the political system into preservation of capital.

The Silencing of Counterweights

This shift didn't happen in a vacuum. For most of the 20th-century, there was a powerful counterweight to corporate political power: **organized labor.** Unions gave working people a collective voice, a shared political megaphone, and a seat at the table where the rules of the economy were written. But as union membership has been deliberately weakened by "right-to-work" laws and court decisions like *Janus v. AFSCME* (2018), which crippled public-sector unions, that balance has collapsed. **Union membership in the U.S. has fallen from over 30% in the 1950s to just 10% today.**

The Auction House, Not the Town Hall

The practical cost is measured in who can even run. A competitive race for a U.S. House seat now costs millions, a Senate seat, tens of millions. **The average winning candidate for the U.S. House spent over $2 million in 2022. For the Senate, it was over $20 million.** Candidates spend up to 70 percent of their time not talking to voters, but calling wealthy donors.

This filters out anyone without a network of wealth or a willingness to become permanently indebted to one. The working-class candidate, the nurse, the teacher, the small business owner, the person who knows what it's like to struggle for the foundations of a good life, are priced out before the race even begins. As the old saying goes, **"The**

first thing to be bought in a campaign is the candidate."

My mother was right about the America we've allowed to evolve. The path to power is paved with gold, not with good ideas or community trust. This means the lived experience of most people, their anxieties about housing, healthcare, and their children's future, is often absent from the rooms where decisions are made.

A Historical Precedent: The Gilded Age & Progressive Fightback

This is not America's first brush with plutocracy. The late 1800s, the Gilded Age, saw a similar fusion of massive corporate wealth (the "robber barons") and political corruption. Senators were sometimes chosen by state legislatures dominated by railroad money. The public reaction was not passive.

This corruption became so brazen that it sparked a powerful, bipartisan backlash. The result was the Tillman Act of 1907, named for its sponsor, Senator "Pitchfork" Ben Tillman. For the first time in American history, it banned all corporate contributions to federal political campaigns.

The law was a direct response to public outrage over corporations like Standard Oil buying influence. It was an imperfect first step, but its principle was revolutionary: a **corporation, a creature of the**

state granted special privileges like limited liability, should not be allowed to use its treasury to control the state that created it. For a time, the Tillman Act stood as a guardrail, acknowledging that corporate money and democratic integrity were fundamentally at odds.

Citizens United didn't just tweak campaign finance; it took a sledgehammer to that century-old guardrail, declaring the dangerous fusion of corporate money and political power to be 'speech.' We are now living with the consequences of that shattered principle.

Out of that muck rose the Progressive Era. A generation of reformers, journalists ("muckrakers"), and activists fought for, and won, landmark changes: the direct election of Senators, antitrust laws, the first campaign finance disclosures, and the federal income tax.

They proved that when democracy is stolen, it can be taken back. They understood that you could not have a republic dedicated to life, liberty, and the pursuit of happiness if it was governed by private monopolies.

We stand at a similar crossroads. *Citizens United* is our era's version of those corrupt Gilded Age practices, a systemic error so profound it demands a political correction.

A Community First Prescription: Reclaiming the Republic

Democracy is not a spectator sport. It is the system we use to build our shared world. Community First Economics demands pro-democracy reforms that are as bold as the threat. We must reclaim the tool of self-government to serve its true purpose: securing the conditions for widespread human prosperity.

Overturn Citizens United & Amplify Real Speech: New Hampshire should join states across the nation in calling for a federal constitutional amendment to clarify that **corporations are not people and money is not speech.**

Publicly Funded Elections to Empower Constituents, Not Donors: Implement a "democracy dollars" or small-donor matching system that amplifies the power of everyday contributions. **Seattle's Democracy Voucher program quadrupled the number of small donors and increased candidate diversity.** If every voter had a "civic credit" to donate to candidates of their choice, politicians would spend their time listening to thousands of constituents, not courting a handful of donors.

Protect and Expand the Right to Vote & Participate: Automatic voter registration, expanded early voting, and making Election Day a state holiday. Make voting easy, secure, and a celebrated civic duty.

Strengthen Countervailing Power: Make it easier, not harder, for workers to organize into unions. A strong labor movement is democracy's best friend, providing the collective voice and power necessary to balance concentrated capital.

The goal is not to eliminate private interests from politics, that's impossible. The goal is to restore the balance, so that the public interest, the community's interest in safe homes, good schools, clean air, and economic security, can be heard above the interests of elites and corporations they own.

My Experience Running for Governor

When I began running for governor, the first issue we ran into was fundraising. I had done a bit of fundraising before, but nothing on the scale this campaign required. I sent out emails, and text messages, soliciting donations, held private dinners in my restaurant and contributed as much of my own money as I could.

Along the process, a thought occurred to me: *the way to get money out of politics was to do politics with as little money as possible.* This became my mantra. The way to remove the donor class's power, was to show campaigns could be run without them.

After the election was over, we had spent about $60,000, most of that going to my campaign manager in the form of a paycheck. At the end of the day we only spent $20,000 on advertising, signs, literature, and stickers. While I lost the primary, I was able to prove that you can have an impact with limited funds. I spent about $4 to $5 per vote. My two competitors each spent $2 million in the same timeframe. That equates to roughly $30 to $35 per vote.

I was able to achieve this by using all the free resources available, mainly social media. Ultimately, people told me that they voted for me because I came across as a normal person, able to speak in a normal fashion. People are tired of the programmed speech most politicians are trained in. I sounded like a human, they sounded like robots.

The Bridge to the Future: Choosing the America We Build

My mother was right about the America we've allowed to exist. But she doesn't have to be right about the America we can build.

Thomas Jefferson warned that "the tree of liberty must be refreshed from time to time," because democracy is a living thing. In America, the health of our democracy should be measured by the strength of our communities and our liberty to pursue happiness.

This corruption of our political system didn't happen in a vacuum. It's the result of a society that has measured success by the wrong scorecard for decades. A system that prioritized the growth of capital over the growth of community. To rebuild a democracy that serves our pursuit of happiness, we must first change what we value and what we measure. We must shift our focus from the abstract metrics of financial extraction to the concrete outcomes of human well-being.

Chapter 8: Education as the Engine & Child Well-Being as Economic Policy

The Ultimate Return on Investment

I was taught from a young age that a democracy cannot survive without educated citizens. If people cannot separate fact from fiction, think critically, or recognize manipulation, the system collapses. I believe we are testing that theory to its breaking point today.

But the stakes are even higher than preserving democracy. **Education is how a society equips each new generation to pursue happiness collectively.** It is the process through which we pass down the tools for understanding the world, the wisdom to navigate it with purpose, and the empathy to do so alongside others. An educated person is more than just a productive worker: they are a capable neighbor, an engaged citizen, a lifelong learner, and a steward of the future.

Our public education system has been systematically underfunded and undermined for decades. The result is a failing of our **intergenerational covenant**. We are neglecting the very machinery through which we renew our society's capacity for innovation, compassion, and growth. Community First Economics sees this with stark clarity: **Education is the single most important infrastructure investment we can make in our community.** It's the engine of opportunity, the guardrail of democracy, and the foundational investment in our community's future vitality.

Let's talk about it like a small business owner would: return on investment.

Study after study shows that money spent on education, especially high-quality early childhood education, pays exponential returns. The famous Perry Preschool Project and ongoing research by economist James Heckman demonstrate that **every dollar invested in early education yields $7 to $12 in long-term benefits** through higher graduation rates, increased lifetime earnings, lower crime, and reduced spending on social services and healthcare.

This is the smartest economic and social development strategy there is. States with strong, well-funded schools have stronger, happier, more resilient communities. They attract businesses that need a skilled and adaptable workforce. They foster innovation because they nurture curious, capable, and collaborative minds. The child in a kindergarten classroom in Claremont is doing more than just learning her ABCs; she's a future nurse, entrepreneur, artist, or engineer who will contribute to our shared prosperity and civic life.

Neglecting this investment is the economics of self-sabotage. It's like eating your seed corn. It's a guaranteed recipe for future scarcity of talent, trust, and social cohesion.

Breaking the Housing Logjam: How School Funding Reform Unlocks Homes

Here is one of the most powerful interconnections in the Community First model, a direct link between the crisis described earlier in the book and the solution: We cannot solve the housing crisis without fixing how we fund our schools.

Right now, towns have a perverse incentive to block affordable housing. Why? Because under our broken property tax system, new families moving into smaller, more affordable homes are seen as a net cost. Their property taxes won't fully cover the expense of educating their children in the local school. So towns use exclusionary zoning to keep them out, protecting their municipal budgets but strangling their communities and fueling the statewide housing shortage.

Community First Economics flips this script. By reforming school funding, shifting the primary responsibility to the state through fair, progressive revenue, we remove the financial fear. A town that welcomes new workforce housing, duplexes, or tiny homes is no longer punished with a fiscal crisis. It can grow organically, confident that the state will ensure its schools are fairly funded through a collective pool of resources.

Fix the school funding formula, and you remove the biggest political barrier to building the homes we desperately need. It's a two-for-one solution for community health: we secure excellent education for every child and open the door to the housing that families and our economy require to thrive.

Learning from the World: And From Mississippi

New Hampshire's hyper-local funding system is an outlier, not just nationally, but globally. Most developed nations treat education as a national or regional responsibility, not a geographical lottery. In countries like Finland, Germany, and Canada, higher levels of government provide the majority of school funding, ensuring a baseline of quality and equity for every child.

In this post World War II era, Finland's rise to the top of global education rankings is widely described as the result of a major pivot away from competition and toward equity and trust. Unlike the American model of high stakes testing and administrative oversight, the Finnish system is built on the professionalization of teaching.

Teachers are trained through research-based university programs and the profession is highly selective and prestigious. Once in the classroom, teachers are granted broad autonomy. There are no national examinations in comprehensive school, there are no teacher ranking systems tied to national tests. The main standardized national exam is the matriculation examination at the end of high school. The system operates on a foundation of high trust, assuming that rigorous preparation reduces the need for bureaucratic policing.

This pedagogical freedom is paired with "a less is more" philosophy that prioritizes the biological and psychological needs of the child. Compulsory schooling begins at age seven, and the school day is commonly structured around shorter lessons with frequent breaks. A typical pattern is forty-five minutes of instruction followed by a fifteen-minute break, which supports movement, reset, and attention.

Homework loads are generally lighter than in many peer countries, especially in earlier grades, and Finland's strongest years in international comparisons have been associated with calm classrooms, focused instruction, and consistently trained teachers rather than test prep culture.

A controversial pillar of the model is how Finland limits private flight. Schooling is tuition-free, and even private providers operate inside a publicly funded, publicly regulated framework. That structure keeps affluent families tied to the same system and helps sustain broad political support for high quality schools everywhere, not only in wealthy neighborhoods. By centering public policy on students rather than the property tax base, Finland aims for the principle that every school should be a good school.

These nations have decided that a child's potential should not be limited by their parents' property value or hometown. They fund schools the same way they fund roads and public safety: as a universal public good essential to the nation's survival, prosperity, and happiness. Their results, in educational attainment, economic mobility, social cohesion, and reported well-being, speak for themselves.

While global models show us the importance of equitable funding, we must also look for practical, evidence-based strategies that work within our classrooms. A powerful example comes from an unexpected place: the state of Mississippi.

For decades, it languished at the bottom of national education rankings. Then, it embarked on a concerted, statewide campaign to improve literacy, with stunning results. **By 2022, Mississippi's 4th graders, once ranked 49th, had risen to tie for 21st in reading on the National Assessment of Educational Progress (NAEP)**—matching the national average and outperforming many wealthier states.

How did they do it? With a Community First-style focus on the foundational skill of reading. The state implemented a multipronged strategy:

The Third-Grade Gate: A law requiring third-graders to demonstrate minimum reading proficiency to advance, creating a systemic imperative to identify and help struggling readers *before* they fell behind.

Investment in the Science of Reading: Retraining thousands of teachers in phonics-based literacy instruction, grounded in cognitive science.

Early Screening and Intensive Intervention: Screening for deficiencies starting in kindergarten, with targeted tutoring and summer literacy camps for those who needed help.

The results speak to a core Community First principle: **prevention is cheaper and more humane than rescue.** Holding a student back for a critical year of literacy intervention is a difficult, short-term cost. But the lifelong cost of functional illiteracy to that individual's pursuit of happiness and to society in lost potential, poverty, and poor health, is incalculably higher. Mississippi chose to make the upfront, foundational investment.

This model offers New Hampshire a crucial lesson. We must have the courage to prioritize **mastery over movement**. Our goal cannot be just to process children through grades. It must be to ensure every child possesses the foundational tools, upon which all future learning and self-determination is built.

Recess and the Woods:
Nature as Essential Educational Infrastructure

Our focus on foundational academic skills must be matched by an equally serious commitment to a child's foundational *human* needs: movement, play, and connection to the natural world. There is a growing body of research that points to a simple, profound, and largely ignored fact: **children learn better, behave better, and feel better when they have regular, unstructured time outdoors.**

Yet, we have systematically stripped this from their school days. Recess has been shortened or used as a bargaining chip. The school day is a marathon of indoor, sedentary concentration. We then medicate and diagnose children for their inability to conform to this unnatural container.

Community First Economics sees this not as a disciplinary issue, but as a design failure. We are trying to build healthy, happy, creative future citizens while denying them the conditions essential for healthy neurological, physical, and social development.

The science is clear:

Cognitive Benefits: Time in nature improves attention, working memory, and cognitive flexibility. **Studies show that children who spend more time outdoors score higher on standardized tests in reading and math.**

Mental Health Benefits: It reduces symptoms of stress, anxiety, and ADHD. It builds resilience.

Physical & Social Benefits: It promotes fitness and fosters negotiation, cooperation, and imagination.

This is an investment in the biological and psychological foundation upon which learning occurs. We would not expect a plant to thrive in a room with no sunlight or fresh air. We must stop expecting it of our children. By reintegrating nature and free movement into the school day, we are not sacrificing academic rigor. We are creating the calm, focused, healthy, and joyful minds that are capable of achieving it. We are building a foundation for lifelong well-being, not just test-taking.

Child Well-Being Is Economic Policy: Cultivating the Seedlings of Our Future

I often see cruel comments aimed at struggling parents, especially single mothers. *If you can't afford kids, you shouldn't have them.* This attitude is not only heartless, it's economically and morally illiterate. It ignores the most fundamental truth there is: Our children are not a private hobby. They are the future.

Human civilization is a relay race. One generation passes the baton to the next. For millennia, societies understood this and invested in their young. That intergenerational contract of care has been in tatters since we decided to treat children as consumer choices rather than as a shared responsibility and our most precious common asset.

Supporting children from birth through adulthood is a strategic investment in our community's most vital infrastructure. When children thrive, towns thrive in perpetuity. When children struggle, we all pay the price for generations, in diminished potential, in reactive spending, and in a frayed social fabric.

This is the essence of Community First Economics: the recognition that the pursuit of happiness is a multigenerational project. We cannot secure our own well-being on the broken backs of our children. Their foundation is our collective foundation.

Childcare: Essential Infrastructure

Let's start with the most obvious market failure: childcare. For too long, we've framed it as a "personal responsibility." But try running a restaurant, a hospital, a factory, or a town when half your workforce can't find or afford safe, nurturing care for their kids. It's impossible.

When my son, Ollie, was born, my restaurant was only one year old. We couldn't afford childcare. His mother and I took turns working in the restaurant and watching the baby. Eventually, his mother got a job as the administrator of our local community church. She brought our son to work with her, where elderly women would dote on him all day as he ran around the sanctuary. We were lucky, saving tens of thousands of dollars we did not have. Most new parents are not so lucky.

Childcare is economic and social infrastructure, as essential as roads or broadband.

Without it, the workforce of today collapses and the workforce of tomorrow is underdeveloped. In New Hampshire, the annual cost of child-care for two children is roughly $32,000.

Meanwhile, the providers, overwhelmingly women, are paid poverty wages, trapped in a broken system that fails everyone.

The Community First solution is straightforward: treat childcare like the public good it is.

•Subsidize access for working families on a sliding scale.

•Invest in the workforce to raise wages and improve quality.

•Integrate services by co-locating childcare centers with senior centers or libraries, fostering cross-generational bonds and creating community hubs of care.

When childcare is stable, affordable, and high-quality, parents can work, businesses can staff, and, most importantly, children get the critical early stimulation, socialization, and security they need for healthy brain development. **High-quality early childcare can increase future earnings by up to 26% and reduce crime rates by 25%.**

Health and Nutrition: The Building Blocks of a Future Citizen

A child who is hungry, lead-poisoned, or battling untreated asthma is a future student who will struggle to concentrate, a future adult with chronic health problems and a future community member with a reduced capacity to contribute and connect. Their pursuit of happiness is compromised before it even begins.

The solutions are simple, proven, and profoundly cost-effective:

School Meals for All: No means-testing, no stigma. Just breakfast and lunch for every student. Children who eat school breakfast have been shown to score 17.5% higher on math tests and attend 1.5 more days of school per year. A child can't learn on an empty stomach.

Protect and Expand Health Coverage: Ensure every child has access to preventative care, dental checkups, and mental health services.

Remove Environmental Toxins: Aggressively test for and remediate lead pipes, PFAS, and mold in homes, schools, and playgrounds.

Every dollar spent on a child's health and nutrition saves seven to ten dollars in future healthcare, special education, criminal justice, and social service costs. This is fiscal responsibility and moral necessity.

The Two-Generation Approach: Supporting Parents is Supporting Kids

Child well-being cannot be separated from family well-being. Stressed, insecure, isolated parents cannot provide stable, nurturing environments. This is why policies like paid family leave, a living wage, and flexible work schedules are child well-being policies.

When parents have time to bond with a newborn without financial panic, income to cover basics without working three jobs, and the flexibility to attend a school conference or care for a sick child, children's outcomes improve dramatically. Children whose parents have access to paid leave are 25% less likely to be hospitalized in their first year of life. We should stop trying to fix children in isolation and invest in the family, caregiving, and community conditions that shape outcomes.

The High Cost of Instability: Foster Care, Homelessness, and Lost Potential

When children are removed from unstable homes or face homelessness, the immediate crisis is only the beginning. The long-term costs of educational disruption, trauma, and systemic dependency are paid by the whole community.

In New Hampshire:

•Over 1,100 children are in foster care, with median stays nearing a year.

•Homelessness among children rose **41% in one year**.

•1 in 4 children live in housing-insecure households.

Nationally, the downstream effects of foster care and childhood instability are staggering:

•**1 in 4 former foster youth** will be incarcerated within two years of aging out of the system.

•**Up to 50%** of youth experiencing homelessness were previously in foster care.

•Only **about half** of foster youth graduate high school by age 19, compared to 87% of their peers.

•Former foster children are **three times more likely** to rely on public assistance as adults.

Why does this matter for education? Because unstable housing and family separation sabotage learning. Children in foster care change schools frequently, fall behind academically, and are far more likely to drop out. Those experiencing homelessness face hunger, stress, and invisibility in the classroom.

But this is more than just a tragedy, it's an economic failure. Foster care costs New Hampshire over **$50 million annually**. Homeless youth often cycle through shelters, emergency healthcare, and later, the criminal justice system. The downstream costs of instability are astronomical.

A Community First Response: Stability as Educational Infrastructure

We cannot educate children who are hungry, homeless, or traumatized by family separation. Therefore, family stability and housing security are **prerequisites for learning**.

A Community First approach recognizes:

Housing support is educational support. Eviction prevention and affordable housing keep families together and kids in school.

Wraparound services keep kids out of foster care. Mental health care, substance treatment, and parenting resources are cheaper and more humane than removal.

Kinship and foster care stability improve outcomes. When kids stay in their communities and schools, they thrive.

Investing in stable housing and family preservation is a fiscally smart move. It reduces future spending on special education, counseling, juvenile justice, and adult incarceration. It transforms vulnerable children into capable students, future workers, and engaged citizens.

In the end, the well-being of children and the strength of our schools depend on the same foundation: **a stable home**. If we want to build a brighter future for New Hampshire, we must start by securing that foundation for every child.

A Covenant with the Future

Skeptics ask, "But how do we pay for it?" We must ask in return: "How can we afford not to?"

The cost of neglect is astronomical and paid in the worst currency:

In Lost Human Potential: Children who start behind rarely catch up. We waste talent and spirit.

In Reactive, Punitive Spending: We skimp on prenatal care, then pay for neonatal intensive care. We defund preschool, then pay for special education. We ignore mental health, then pay for incarceration.

In Community Erosion: Families in constant crisis can't volunteer or invest in their neighborhoods. The social fabric tears, trust evaporates.

Investing in children is the opposite of a handout. It is a hand-up to the entire community across time. It creates a virtuous cycle: healthy, educated, socially-skilled children become a resilient, innovative, and compassionate workforce and citizenry. This attracts business, broadens the tax base, and creates a society where people want to live and raise their own families.

Schools are where children from different backgrounds learn and play together, forging the bonds of a common identity. They are where parents meet, where town voting happens, where disaster shelters are set up. They are the heartbeat of the town.

This is more than policy. It is a covenant. A promise that we will not punish children for the circumstances of their birth. A promise that we value them not merely for their future economic output, but for their inherent humanity and their role as the next stewards of our world.

Investing in education and child well-being is the ultimate act of faith in our children and in each other. It is how we ensure that the pursuit of happiness is not a privilege for the lucky few, but a cultivated capacity for all. Let's build a foundation worthy of that faith, and in doing so, rebuild the most powerful engine of our common prosperity and shared happiness.

Chapter 9:
How Health Care Became a Corporate System and How We Take It Back

The American health care system did not become the most expensive system in the world overnight. It became this way through a series of policy choices that slowly moved care away from communities and into corporate control.

What makes this especially frustrating is that we once had something closer to a community-based model. It was imperfect, but it was community-based care. Over time, we replaced that model with layers of insurance middlemen, financial incentives, and consolidation. Today, patients feel trapped, doctors feel burned out, and taxpayers are paying more than ever for outcomes that lag behind other wealthy countries.

Community First Economics is about reversing systems that drifted away from their original purpose, and guiding them back to a goal of healing. What's the point of curing disease if it means leaving the patient crippled with debt?

When Health Care Was Local

For most of American history, health care worked much like any other local service. You went to a doctor in your town. You paid directly, often in cash. Hospitals were usually nonprofit institutions, many run by religious or community organizations. Insurance, where it existed, was designed to cover rare and expensive hospital stays, not to micromanage everyday care.

In small New England towns, this model survived longer than in big cities. Local hospitals, local physicians, and community trust mattered. The system was not equal, many people were left out, but it was not yet dominated by national corporations or opaque pricing systems.

How Insurance Started as Nonprofit Risk-Sharing

Modern health insurance did not begin as a profit engine. Early health insurance plans were nonprofit prepayment systems created to stabilize hospitals and protect families from catastrophic bills. The original Blue Cross model was built around community hospitals and nonprofit principles.

The core idea was simple: everyone pays a small amount. When someone gets sick, the community pool covers the cost. No one was trying to extract shareholder returns from the process.

That idea matters because it shows something important: health insurance was originally meant to serve communities, not dominate them.

The Decision That Changed Everything: Tying Health Insurance to Jobs

The biggest turning point in American healthcare had nothing to do with medicine.

During World War Two, the federal government imposed wage controls. Employers could not compete for workers by raising pay, so they started offering benefits instead. Health insurance became the most attractive option. Later, tax policy locked this in by making employer-provided health insurance tax-advantaged.

That decision reshaped American life.

Health care became tied to employment rather than residency or citizenship. Leaving a job meant risking the loss of coverage. Small businesses were placed at a disadvantage compared to large corporations. Workers lost leverage. Families lost stability. How many people are currently suffering at a job they hate because they "need the benefits"?

This is one of the least market-based systems imaginable. Consumers do not choose their insurance freely. They inherit it from their employer. Prices are hidden. Networks are imposed. Care decisions are filtered through corporate profit motives.

Medicare and Medicaid: A Moral Breakthrough

The creation of Medicare and Medicaid was a moral breakthrough. We decided that seniors and low-income families should not be abandoned.

But instead of replacing the fragmented system, we layered public programs on top of it. That created a patchwork of coverage types, payment rules, billing systems, and administrative complexity.

Doctors and hospitals now deal with dozens of payers, each with different rules. That complexity is not an accident. It is a business model.

Why Costs Exploded

The crisis we face today has several overlapping causes:

Aging Population: Baby boomers are entering the years when health care use rises sharply. This is real, and it puts pressure on any system.

Workforce Shortages: We do not have enough doctors and nurses. Burnout is widespread. Rural areas and smaller states like New Hampshire feel this acutely. When care is scarce, it becomes expensive.

Consolidation: Hospitals merge. Insurance companies merge.

Physician practices get bought by large systems. When competition shrinks, prices rise. Communities lose control.

What the Affordable Care Act Fixed (and What It Did Not)

The Affordable Care Act expanded coverage and protected people with preexisting conditions. That matters, and it should not be dismissed.

But it did not change the underlying structure of health care financing. In some ways, it reinforced it.

Compliance costs, reporting requirements, and standardized benefit rules made it easier for large insurers and hospital systems to survive and harder for smaller ones. Consolidation continued. Administrative overhead grew. Prices kept rising.

The Affordable Care Act treated the symptoms without addressing the disease. The disease is a system built around insurance middlemen rather than care.

The Core Problem: Too Many Toll Booths Between Patient and Provider

In the current system, insurance companies are no longer just insuring against catastrophic risk. They sit between patients and clinicians in routine care, shaping decisions through prior authorizations, network restrictions, and billing rules.

This creates a vicious cycle:

- Providers hire billing staff to fight insurers.

- Insurers hire staff to manage denials.

- Hospitals raise prices to survive.

- Employers pass costs to workers.

- Government subsidies grow just to keep coverage affordable.

Everyone pays more, except the people extracting value from complexity.

A Community First Path Forward

We do not need to burn the system down. We need to simplify it, rebuild capacity, and shift power back to communities.

Community Health Clinics with Direct Payment: One solution is expanding community health clinics where patients pay clinicians directly for routine care, with transparent pricing and public support.

Primary care, preventive care, behavioral health, and chronic disease management should not require navigating an insurance maze. Insurance should return to its original purpose: protecting against major, unpredictable costs.

To make this equitable, clinics must be publicly supported, with sliding-scale fees and strong rural access. This is not a boutique model. It is infrastructure.

More Doctors and Nurses, Trained and Kept Locally: Coverage without capacity is an illusion. We need more residency slots, more training partnerships, and real incentives for clinicians to practice in New Hampshire and New England. Loan forgiveness tied to service, better working conditions, and team-based care are essential. This should be treated like building roads or power lines. A health workforce is public infrastructure.

A New England Public Insurance Option: Here is where Community First Economics becomes practical. New Hampshire already helps pay for health insurance for state employees, teachers, and first responders. Right now, much of that money flows through private insurers.

Instead, we could create a public, nonprofit insurance plan that directly pays providers with simple, transparent rates. Start with public employees. That creates a stable risk pool.

Then allow small businesses, self-employed workers, and individuals to buy in voluntarily. That breaks the link between employment and coverage without forcing anyone out of their existing plan.

Over time, this could expand regionally across New England. Our labor markets already cross state lines. Our hospital systems already operate regionally. Our insurance system should reflect how people actually live.

Has This Been Tried Before?

State-level single-payer has been attempted, most notably in Vermont, and failed largely due to financing challenges and political resistance. That is an important lesson: sudden, total replacement is risky.

But incremental public options have worked in multiple states. Internationally, countries like Taiwan and Germany show that you can finance care publicly while keeping providers private, controlling costs without sacrificing access.

The lesson is not that reform is impossible. The lesson is that reform works best when it grows from systems people already trust.

The Promise of Community First Health Care

Health care should not feel like a financial trap. It should feel like a public good that supports families, workers, and small businesses.

A Community First approach does not ask whether health care is socialist or capitalist. It asks whether it works.

- Does it keep people healthy?

- Does it let doctors practice medicine?

- Does it strengthen communities instead of draining them?

If the answer is no, then the system needs to change.

Health care is not a commodity like cable television. It is the foundation of economic security. When people are healthy and stable, communities thrive. When they are not, everything else falls apart. Community First Economics starts with that simple truth, and builds from there.

Chapter 10: A New Social Contract From GDP to Gross National Happiness

> "Economic growth has not brought a rise in happiness. That is the paradox of modern society."
> – Richard Easterlin

For eighty years, this country has measured its success with one number: Gross Domestic Product. GDP counts every monetary transaction. It counts the sale of an opioid and the prison built to house the addict. It counts the cancer treatment, but not the health of the patient. It goes up after a hurricane, when we spend billions rebuilding what was lost. It celebrates the fever, not the recovery.

Since 1970, U.S. GDP has tripled, yet the percentage of Americans reporting they are "very happy" has declined. GDP measures activity. It does not measure **well-being**.

And because we manage what we measure, we have built a society that is very good at generating economic activity, and very bad at generating security, connection, and dignity.

The Pursuit of Happiness Needs a Scorecard

If the purpose of our economy, the management of our shared household, is to create the conditions for the pursuit of happiness, then we must use a different scorecard.

This is not a radical idea. It is the oldest idea.

For most of human history, communities measured wealth in health, in shared harvests, in the strength of their children, and in the wisdom of their elders. The shift to measuring everything in dollars is a recent, and catastrophic, narrowing of vision.

The good news is that a correction is already underway in the world. In the 1970s, the king of Bhutan declared that **"Gross National Happiness is more important than Gross National Product."** They built a national policy around four pillars: sustainable development, environmental conservation, cultural preservation, and good governance. They began to measure loneliness, time spent with family, trust in neighbors, and connection to nature.

Bhutan now ranks among the happiest countries in Asia, despite having a GDP per capita one-twentieth that of the United States.

In 2019, New Zealand's Prime Minister Jacinda Ardern stood before her nation and unveiled the world's first "well-being Budget." She said,

"We're measuring our success not just by the state of our finances, but by the state of our people." The treasury now allocates billions based on five priorities: mental health, child poverty, indigenous reconciliation, digital inclusion, and a low-carbon economy. They are measuring what matters.

These nations have made a profound discovery: **what you measure dictates what you prioritize.** If you only count dollars, you will prioritize the movement of dollars. If you count well-being, you will build the foundations of well-being.

The New Hampshire Well-Being Index: A Blueprint for Our Future

We don't have to wait for Washington. We can do this here. In fact, we must.

New Hampshire could become the first state in America to officially adopt a Well-Being Index to guide our budget, our laws, and our vision for the future. This would be the ultimate expression of "Live Free or Die", not as a slogan of neglect, but as a promise: *we will create the conditions where every person has the security to truly live free.*

Imagine the Governor standing before the General Court, not just with a financial budget, but with a **well-being Report**. It would track things like:

The Housing Security Rate: The percentage of residents spending less than 30% of their income on shelter.

The Childhood Belonging Index: Measured through surveys of schoolchildren about whether they feel safe, known, and supported.

The Senior Connection Score: Tracking social isolation among residents over 65.

The Community Trust Metric: How many people know their neighbors, volunteer, or trust local government.

The Mental Health of Our Youth: Rates of anxiety, depression, and hope among teenagers.

Every line item in the state budget would then be evaluated against a simple question: **Will this improve our Well-Being Index?**

That new question changes everything.

Suddenly, funding for school counselors isn't a "cost." It's an investment in the Childhood Belonging Index and the Mental Health of Our Youth.

Building accessory dwelling units isn't a zoning nuisance. It's an investment in the Housing Security Rate *and* the Senior Connection Score.

A living wage isn't a "burden on business." It's the most direct way to improve nearly every metric of family well-being.

The Virtuous Cycle:
How Measuring Well-Being Fixes Our Systems

This shift in measurement is more than just symbolic. It's the master key that unlocks the logjams in all our other systems.

Take housing and schools, the twin crises choking our towns.

Right now, a town looks at a proposal for a new duplex and sees a fiscal threat. Under our broken property tax system, new families mean more children in schools, which means higher local taxes. So the town says no. It zones for exclusion to protect its budget.

But under a Well-Being Index, that same duplex is seen as a **well-being asset**. It improves the Housing Security Rate for two families. It adds to the town's economic resilience and social fabric. And because school funding is tied to statewide well-being goals the town is no longer financially punished for growing. The fear is removed. The logjam breaks.

A seminal study in *Science* found that neighborhoods with higher levels of trust and shared expectations for control, a measure called 'collective efficacy', experienced up to 40% fewer homicides, regardless of their economic disadvantage.

The Economics of Happiness: Not a Cost, but a Dividend

Skeptics will ask the old question: *"But how do we pay for it?"*

We must ask the new question: *"How much do we pay for not doing it?"*

The cost of our current system, the one that only measures GDP, is astronomical. We pay for it in:

The prison cells we build instead of preschool classrooms. **The U.S. spends over $80 billion annually on incarceration; more than double what it spends on Pell Grants for college students.**

The emergency room visits we fund instead of preventative care.

The lost productivity of parents who can't work because they can't find childcare.

The broken social fabric of towns where no one has time to volunteer because they're working three jobs.

Study after study shows that investments in well-being yield staggering returns. For low-income children, every $1 invested in preschool yields

$8.60 in long-term public benefits through reduced crime, welfare, and health costs. Every dollar spent on lead pipe removal saves $10 in future healthcare and special education costs. Every dollar that prevents a senior from falling into isolation saves countless more in medical and eldercare expenses.

Focusing on future happiness is not a luxury. It is the ultimate fiscal responsibility.

A Covenant with the Future

This book began with a burger and a fact: when people have economic security, they invest in their community.

We have traveled through the systems that steal that security: the housing trap, the property tax squeeze, the corporation that turned from public tool to private power, the democracy auctioned to the highest bidder and a broken medical system.

Each of those systems is a choice. We built them. We can rebuild them.

The pursuit of happiness is not a solo sprint. It is a relay race across generations. Our parents and grandparents passed us a baton; a promise of liberty, a chance to build a good life on a foundation of security.

Now it is our turn to run our leg of the race. Our task is not just to pass the baton, but to repair the track.

A New Hampshire Well-Being Index is more than a policy. It is a **covenant**. A promise that we will measure our success by the strength of our people and the health of our places. A promise that we will count what counts.

We are not a poor state. We are a rich community that has been using the wrong tool to measure the health of our society. Let's build an economy that remembers its purpose: to manage our shared household so that everyone in the house can thrive.

The future is not something that happens to us. It is something we create, something we build, and something we choose together.

Let's get to work.

The End

I closed Jonny Boston's for good in the second week of July 2025. I could no longer fulfill my goal of selling tasty, affordable food to my local community. I could not, in good conscience, sell a steak burrito for $18, which the current economic conditions demanded. I knew that the system was fundamentally broken, and my energy would be best spent championing a new way of running our state. We need a new system that does not cripple residents with excessive property tax bills, allows everyone access to housing and gives every child a chance to succeed.

I was tired of making more sales every year but less profit. I was tired of feeling like the government did not value the unmeasured benefits of having restaurants, breweries, and cafés. The relationship building that happens in these third spaces is essential for community development and cohesion.

The other day my son said, "Dad, can we open up a restaurant together when I finish school?" And I said yes. He is nine years old, so that gives me about eight years to fight for a world in which my son can operate a restaurant and not have to worry about health insurance, housing, or regressive taxes.

I am fighting for the future because I love my son. I want him to have the same chance to pursue happiness that previous generations of

Americans did. We owe it to our children to do the work to ensure they inherit a world worth living in and that starts when we begin to put our community first.

You can learn more about Jon Kiper's run for governor of New Hampshire at **VoteKiper.org**

Endnotes and Sources

Introduction & Chapter 1: The Big Kahuna

Economic Policy Institute, "The Productivity–Pay Gap," updated 2023, https://www.epi.org/productivity-pay-gap/.

Pew Research Center, "How the American Middle Class Has Changed in the Past Five Decades," April 20, 2022, https://www.pewresearch.org/short-reads/2022/04/20/how-the-american-middle-class-has-changed-in-the-past-five-decades/.

New Hampshire Housing Finance Authority / New Hampshire Association of REALTORS®, "New Hampshire Housing Market Data — 2023," https://nhar-public.stats.showingtime.com/docs/ann/x/StatewideOnly?src=map.

Institute on Taxation and Economic Policy, Who Pays? 7th Edition, https://itep.org/whopays/.

USAFacts, "Who Owns American Wealth? The Top 1% Hold 30% of Net Worth," November 2023, https://usafacts.org/articles/who-owns-american-wealth/.

Chapter 2: What is Community First Economics?

New Hampshire Housing Finance Authority, "Who Can Afford to Live in New Hampshire? Housing Market Update," October 5, 2025, https://www.nhhfa.org/who-can-afford-to-live-in-new-hampshire/.

Economic Policy Institute, "Wages Have Grown More for the Top 1% Than the Bottom 90% Over Decades," https://www.epi.org/publication/charting-wage-stagnation/.

Economic Policy Institute, "CEO Pay Has Skyrocketed 1,460% Since 1978," October 4, 2022, https://www.epi.org/publication/ceo-pay-in-2021/.

RAND Corporation, "A $2.5 Trillion Question: What If Incomes Grew Like GDP Did?" commentary, October 6, 2020, https://www.rand.org/pubs/commentary/2020/10/a-25-trillion-question-what-if-incomes-grew-like-gdp.html.

S&P Dow Jones Indices, "S&P 500 Q4 2022 Buybacks Tick up, As 2022 Sets A Record," press release, March 21, 2023, https://press.spglobal.com/2023-03-21-S-P-500-Q4-2022-Buybacks-Tick-up,-As-2022-Sets-A-Record.

Chapter 3: The Disappearing Middle Class

Pew Research Center, "Almost 1 in 5 Stay-at-Home Parents in the

U.S. Are Dads," August 3, 2023, https://www.pewresearch.org/short-reads/2023/08/03/almost-1-in-5-stay-at-home-parents-in-the-us-are-dads/.

Pew Research Center, "Breadwinner Wives and Mothers," full report, April 13, 2023, https://www.pewresearch.org/wp-content/uploads/sites/20/2023/04/Breadwinner-wives-full-report-FINAL.pdf.

New Hampshire Association of REALTORS®, "New Hampshire Single-Family Residential Home Sales, Statewide: 1998 to Present," accessed February 2026, https://nhar-public.stats.showingtime.com/docs/ann/x/StatewideOnly?src=map. T

U.S. Census Bureau, "Historical Median Household Income by State, Current Population Survey (Table H-8) and American Community Survey 1-Year Estimates (New Hampshire)," accessed February 2026, https://www.census.gov/data/tables/time-series/demo/income-poverty/historical-income-households.html. (1998-2024).

KFF (Kaiser Family Foundation), 2023 Employer Health Benefits Survey, October 18, 2023, https://www.kff.org/health-costs/2023-employer-health-benefits-survey/.

U.S. Bureau of Labor Statistics, Consumer Price Index Inflation

Calculator, accessed

February 2026, https://www.bls.gov/data/inflation_calculator.htm.

New Hampshire Fiscal Policy Institute, "High Prices and Low Availability of Child Care in New Hampshire: Challenges Continue," January 14, 2025, https://nhfpi.org/resource/high-prices-and-low-availability-of-child-care-in-new-hampshire-challenges-continue-in-2025/.

The Institute for College Access & Success, "Student Debt for College Graduates in New Hampshire," accessed February 2026, https://ticas.org/new-hampshire/.

U.S. Federal Reserve Board, Report on the Economic Well-Being of U.S. Households in 2024 (May 2025), Section 5, https://www.federalreserve.gov/publications/2025-economic-well-being-of-us-households.htm.

Brookings Institution, "The Middle-Class Time Squeeze," August 18, 2020, https://www.brookings.edu/wp-content/uploads/2020/08/The-Middle-Class-Time-Squeeze_08.18.2020.pdf.

Gu, Y., et al., "Income Inequality and Political Polarization," Journal of Chinese Political Science (2022): 105728, https://pmc.ncbi.nlm.nih.gov/articles/PMC8608558/.

Chapter 4: The Housing Crisis & The Path Home

New Hampshire Housing Finance Authority, 2023 Statewide Housing Needs Assessment, March 2023, https://www.nhhfa.org/wp-content/uploads/2023/04/2023-NH-Statewide-Housing-Needs-Assessment.pdf.

New Hampshire Housing Finance Authority, 2023 Statewide Housing Needs Assessment– Executive Summary, March 2023, https://www.nhhfa.org/wp-content/uploads/2023/04/2023-NH-Statewide-Housing-Needs-Assessment-Executive-Summary.pdf.

State of New Hampshire, Department of Business and Economic Affairs, New Hampshire Economic and Housing Report 2024, https://www.nheconomy.com/getmedia/13040d3b-0f35-4bd9-bb7c-f204d9e6ac07/2024-Housing-Report.pdf.

Collinson, Robert, and Peter Ganong, "How Do Changes in Housing Voucher Design Affect Rent and Neighborhood Quality?" American Economic Journal: Economic Policy 10, no. 2 (2018), https://www.aeaweb.org/articles?id=10.1257/pol.20150176.

Harvard Joint Center for Housing Studies, The State of the Nation's Housing 2022, https://www.jchs.harvard.edu/state-nations-housing-2022.

Richard Rothstein, "Suppressed History: The Intentional Segregation of America's Cities," American Educator, Spring 2021.

U.S. Department of Housing and Urban Development, HOPE VI Data Compilation and Analysis, 2016, https://www.huduser.gov/portal/sites/default/files/pdf/HOPE-VI-Data-Compilation-and-Analysis.pdf. Nationwide, HOPE VI demolished about 98,592 public housing units.

International Housing Solutions (HOUSE-IN), Vienna Case Study,

https://www.ufz.de/export/data/2/261384_

HOUSEIN_CaseStudyProfile_Vienna.pdf.

RiverBay Corporation, "About Co-op City," https://www.coopcity.com/aboutus/.

Singapore Department of Statistics, "Resident Households," https://www.singstat.gov.sg/find-data/search-by-theme/households/resident-households.

Government of Singapore, "Evolution of Public Housing in Singapore," https://www.gov.sg/explainers/evolution-of-public-housing-in-singapore/.

Champlain Housing Trust, Annual Report 2024, https://www.getahome.org/wp-content/uploads/AnnualReport_202

4.pdf.

National League of Cities, "Community Land Trusts: A Guide for Local Governments," https://www.nlc.org/resource/community-land-trusts-a-guide-for-local-governments/.

Vox, "Tokyo's Housing Miracle Explains Why the U.S. Has a Housing Crisis," August 8, 2016, https://www.vox.com/2016/8/8/12390048/san-francisco-housing-costs-tokyo.

New Hampshire Revised Statutes Annotated, RSA 162-A:22, "Unified Contingent Credit Limit," https://law.justia.com/codes/new-hampshire/title-xii/chapter-162-a/section-162-a-22/.

New Hampshire Business Finance Authority, "Real Estate Development," https://nhbfa.com/real-estate-development/.

Freddie Mac, "Housing Supply: A Growing Deficit," May 7, 2021, https://www.freddiemac.com/research/insight/20210507-housing-supply.

USAFacts, "Households Paying More Than 30 Percent of Income on Housing – New Hampshire," https://usafacts.org/answers/how-many-households-in-the-united-states-spend-too-much-on-housing/state/new-hampshire/.

Chapter 5: The Property Tax & A Fair Funding System

Lincoln Institute of Land Policy, Significant Features of the Property Tax: New Hampshire (2020; data updated October 2023), https://www.lincolninst.edu/app/uploads/legacy-files/nh_october_2023.pdf.

Institute on Taxation and Economic Policy, Who Pays? 7th Edition, https://itep.org/whopays/.

New Hampshire Fiscal Policy Institute, "New Hampshire State Funding Rate for Public Elementary and Secondary Education Lowest in Nation," December 7, 2023, https://nhfpi.org/resource/new-hampshire-state-funding-rate-for-public-elementary-and-secondary-education-lowest-in-nation/.

New Hampshire Department of Education, Bureau of Education Statistics, "Financial Reports: Cost Per Pupil by District," https://www.education.nh.gov/who-we-are/division-of-educator-and-analytic-resources/bureau-of-education-statistics/financial-reports.

Jackson, C. Kirabo, Rucker C. Johnson, and Claudia Persico, "The Effects of School Spending on Educational and Economic Outcomes: Evidence from School Finance Reforms," NBER Working Paper 20847 (January 2015), https://www.nber.org/system/files/working_papers/w20847/w20847.pdf.

New Hampshire Fiscal Policy Institute, "Households with High Incomes Disproportionately Benefit from Interest and Dividends Tax Repeal," March 14, 2023, https://nhfpi.org/blog/households-with-high-incomes-disproportionately-benefit-from-interest-and-dividends-tax-repeal/. About 92% of the dollars from eliminating the

Chapter 6: The Myth of the Self-Made Millionaire & The Rise of

the Corporation

Internet Society, "A Brief History of the Internet,"

https://www.internetsociety.org/internet/history-internet/brief-history-internet/. Accessed February 3, 2026.

National Science Foundation, "NSF and the Internet: An Overview,"

https://www.nsf.gov/news/special_reports/nsfnet/. Accessed February 3, 2026. CERN, "The Birth of the Web," https://home.cern/science/computing/birth-web. Accessed February 3, 2026.

Federal Highway Administration, "Happy 40th Anniversary, Interstate Highway System,"
https://highways.dot.gov/highway-history/interstate-system/happy-4

0th-anniversary-interstate-highway-system.

Freight Analysis Framework, "Freight Analysis Framework Data Tabulation Tool," Oak Ridge National Laboratory, https://faf.ornl.gov/faf5/dtt.

Lee Fleming, Hillary Greene, Guan-Cheng Li, Matt Marx, and Dennis Yao, "Government-Funded Research Increasingly Fuels Innovation," Science 364, no. 6446 (2019): 1139-1141.

Francis Narin et al., "Patents and Publicly Funded Research," in Assessing the Value of Research in the Chemical Sciences (Washington, DC: National Academies Press, 1998), chapter 6.

Thomas Jefferson to George Logan, November 12, 1816, in The Papers of Thomas Jefferson, Retirement Series, vol. 10, May 1816 to January 1817, ed. J. Jefferson Looney (Princeton: Princeton University Press, 2013), 532. Available at Founders Online:

https://founders.archives.gov/documents/Jefferson/03-10-02-0390.

U.S. Supreme Court, Dartmouth College v. Woodward, 17 U.S. 518 (1819), https://supreme.justia.com/cases/federal/us/17/518/.

Michigan Supreme Court, Dodge v. Ford Motor Co., 204 Mich. 459 (1919),

https://law.justia.com/cases/michigan/supreme-court/1919/204-

mich-459-170-n-w-668-1919.html.

Tax Policy Center (Urban Institute and Brookings Institution), Historical Corporate Top Tax Rate and Bracket, Tax Years 1909-2024, https://taxpolicycenter.org/statistics/historical-corporate-income-tax-rates.

Markus Krajewski, "The Great Lightbulb Conspiracy," IEEE Spectrum, September 24, 2014, https://spectrum.ieee.org/the-great-lightbulb-conspiracy.

U.S. Environmental Protection Agency, "Plastics: Material-Specific Data,"

https://www.epa.gov/facts-and-figures-about-materials-waste-and-recycling/plastics-material-specific-data.

Danny Yagan, "What Is the Average Federal Individual Income Tax Rate on the Wealthiest Americans?" Working paper, University of California, Berkeley, https://eml.berkeley.edu/~yagan/wealthtaxrates.pdf.

Cato Institute, "Corporate Welfare in the Federal Budget," https://www.cato.org/policy-analysis/corporate-welfare-federal-budget.

Franklin D. Roosevelt, "Address at Madison Square Garden, New

York City," speech delivered October 31, 1936, The American Presidency Project, https://www.presidency.ucsb.edu/documents/address-madison-square-garden-new-york-city.

Mondragon Corporation, "Mondragon at a Glance," https://www.mondragon-corporation.com/en/about-us/.

Chapter 7: The Price of Democracy

U.S. Supreme Court, Citizens United v. Federal Election Commission, 558 U.S. 310 (2010).

OpenSecrets, "By the Numbers: 15 Years of Citizens United," January 27, 2025,

https://www.opensecrets.org/news/2025/01/by-the-numbers-15-years-of-citizens-united/.

Brennan Center for Justice, "Citizens United, Explained," https://www.brennancenter.org/our-work/research-reports/citizens-united-explained.

Center for American Progress, "Undoing Citizens United and Reining in Super PACs," https://www.americanprogress.org/article/undoing-citizens-united-and-reining-in-super-pacs/. more than $4.2 billion.

U.S. Bureau of Labor Statistics, "Union Members Summary,"

Economic News Release, annual series, https://www.bls.gov/news.release/union2.nr0.htm.

U.S. Supreme Court, Janus v. American Federation of State, County, and Municipal. Employees, Council 31, 585 U.S. ___, 138 S. Ct. 2448 (2018).

OpenSecrets, "Cost of Election," https://www.opensecrets.org/elections-overview/cost-of-election.

Chapter 8: Education as the Engine & Child Well-Being as Economic Policy

James J. Heckman, "The Economics of Human Potential," Heckman Equation, 2023, https://heckmanequation.org.

National Center for Education Statistics, "NAEP 2022 Reading Results," 2022,

https://www.nationsreportcard.gov/reading/nation/achievement/.

Frontiers in Psychology, "The Benefits of Outdoor Play," 2019,

https://doi.org/10.3389/fpsyg.2019.00305.

Gray-Lobe, Guthrie, Parag A. Pathak, and Christopher R. Walters,

"The Long-Term Effects of Universal Preschool in Boston," NBER Working Paper 28756 (May 2021),

https://www.nber.org/papers/w28756.

Share Our Strength, No Kid Hungry Annual Report 2024 (Our Impact), https://annualreport.nokidhungry.org/.

Pac, Jessica, Maya Rossin-Slater, Jenna Steingruebner, et al., "Paid Family Leave and Parental Investments in Infant Health: Evidence from California," Economics & Human Biology 48 (2023), https://doi.org/10.1016/j.ehb.2023.101283.

New Hampshire Public Radio, "Points of Progress, Grim Statistics Shape NH Child Advocate's Annual Report," February 6, 2023, https://www.nhpr.org/nh-news/2023-02-06/points-of-progress-grim-statistics-shape-nh-child-advocates-annual-report.

New Hampshire Public Radio, "In Manchester, an Urgent Call to Address NH's Rising Youth Homelessness: 'See Our Faces,'" March 24, 2025, https://www.nhpr.org/nh-news/2025-03-24/in-manchester-an-urgent-call-to-address-nhs-rising-youth-homelessness-see-our-faces.

NH Coalition to End Homelessness, "State of Homelessness in New Hampshire Annual Report 2024,"

https://www.nhceh.org/news/nhceh-state-of-homelessness-in-new-hampshire-annual-report-shows-continued-increases-in-nh-homelessness/. Sanctuary of Hope, "Foster Youth Statistics - The Need," October 30, 2020,

https://thesoh.org/about-us/foster-youth-statistics-need/.

Amy Dworsky, Laura Napolitano, and Mark Courtney, "Homelessness During the Transition From Foster Care to Adulthood," American Journal of Public Health 103, no.

S2 (2013): S318-S323, https://pmc.ncbi.nlm.nih.gov/articles/PMC3969135/.

Youth.gov, "Child Welfare System," https://youth.gov/youth-topics/homelessness-and-housing-instability/child-welfare-system.

Christian Alliance for Orphans, "US Foster Care Statistics 2025," November 10, 2025, https://cafo.org/foster-care-statistics/.

Protopsaltis, Spiros, and Sharon Parrott, "Pell Grants — A Key Tool for Expanding College Access and Economic Opportunity — Need Strengthening, Not Cuts," Center on Budget and Policy Priorities, July 27, 2017, https://www.cbpp.org/research/federal-budget/pell-grants-a-key-tool-for-expanding-college-access-and-economic.

Bureau of Justice Statistics, "Prisoners in 2022," 2023,

https://bjs.ojp.gov/library/publications/prisoners-2022-statistical-tables.

Chapter 9: How Health Care Became a Corporate System and How We Take It Back

Blue Cross Blue Shield Association, "History of Blue Cross Blue Shield," https://www.bcbs.com/about-us/blue-cross-history-of-healthcare.

Robert Cunningham III and Robert M. Cunningham Jr., The Blues: A History of the Blue Cross and Blue Shield System (DeKalb: Northern Illinois University Press, 1997). Stabilization Act of 1942, Pub. L. 77-729, 56 Stat. 765 (October 2, 1942).

David Balat, "The employer-health insurance connection an 'accident of history,'" The Hill, November 9, 2019, https://thehill.com/opinion/healthcare/469739-the-employer-health-insurance-connection-an-accident-of-history/.

PeopleKeep, "The Complete History of Employer-Provided Health Insurance,"

https://www.peoplekeep.com/blog/the-complete-history-of-employer-provided-health-insurance.

Social Security Amendments of 1965, Pub. L. 89-97, 79 Stat. 286 (July

30, 1965). Centers for Medicare & Medicaid Services, "History," https://www.cms.gov/about-cms/agency-information/history.

Patient Protection and Affordable Care Act, Pub. L. 111-148, 124 Stat. 119 (March 23, 2010).

NPR, "Why Bernie Sanders' Single-Payer Health Care Plan Failed In Vermont," September 13, 2017, https://www.npr.org/2017/09/13/550757713/why-bernie-sanders-single-payer-health-care-plan-failed-in-vermont.

Chapter 10: A New Social Contract – From GDP to Gross

National Happiness Nicholas H. Wolfinger, "Young Adult Happiness From 1990 to 2022 Is Down a Bit. Why?"

Institute for Family Studies, December 12, 2023, https://ifstudies.org/blog/young-adult-happiness-from-1990-to-2022-is-down-a-bit-why.

World Happiness Report, "Bhutan and Gross National Happiness," 2023,

https://worldhappiness.report. Bhutan now ranks among the happiest countries in Asia.

New Zealand Treasury, "The well-being Budget 2019," May 30, 2019, https://www.treasury.govt.nz/publications/well-being-budget/well-being-budget-2019.

OECD, How's Life? 2020: Measuring Well-Being – Highlights, March 2020,

https://www.oecd.org/sdd/How-is-Life-2020-Highlights.pdf.

Robert J. Sampson, Stephen W. Raudenbush, and Felton Earls, "Neighborhoods and

Violent Crime: A Multilevel Study of Collective Efficacy," Science 277, no. 5328 (1997): 918-924.

The Pew Charitable Trusts, Cutting Lead Poisoning and Public Costs, issue brief, December 2010,

https://www.pewtrusts.org/~/media/assets/2010/12/14/cutting_lead_poisoning_brief.pdf.

van Bavel, Rens, et al., "Social Capital as a Protective Resource in Times of Social Crisis— Lessons from the COVID-19 Pandemic," Frontiers in Public Health 10 (2022),

https://doi.org/10.3389/fpubh.2022.1037395.

General Further Exploration

Thomas Piketty, Capital in the Twenty-First Century (Harvard University Press, 2014)

Matthew Desmond, Evicted: Poverty and Profit in the American City (Crown, 2016)

Jane Jacobs, The Death and Life of Great American Cities (Random House, 1961)

Kate Raworth, Doughnut Economics: Seven Ways to Think Like a 21st-Century Economist (Chelsea Green, 2017)

Rutger Bregman, Utopia for Realists (Little, Brown, 2017)

Heather McGhee, The Sum of Us: What Racism Costs Everyone and How We Can Prosper Together (One World, 2021)

New Hampshire Fiscal Policy Institute: https://nhfpi.org

NH Housing Finance Authority Research: https://www.nhhfa.org/research

The Brookings Institution: https://www.brookings.edu

Economic Policy Institute: https://www.epi.org

OECD Well-being Reports: https://www.oecd.org/wise

www.ingramcontent.com/pod-product-compliance
Lightning Source LLC
Chambersburg PA
CBHW020544030426
42337CB00013B/972